THE BURNT CHILD

THE BURNT CHILD

An Autobiography

by

EDWARD LUCIE-SMITH

LONDON
VICTOR GOLLANCZ LTD
1975

ISBN 0 575 01925 5

Printed in Great Britain by
The Camelot Press Ltd, Southampton

For Deborah and Pat
good angels

ACKNOWLEDGEMENT

Chapters Seventeen and Eighteen in this book originally appeared in slightly different form in the anthology *All Bull* edited by Bryan Johnson (Allison and Busby, 1973).

CHAPTER ONE

THE FIRST THING that I know I remember clearly is a small chromium-plated buckle. I open my eyes, and it swims into focus. It is attached to a thin strap, and this strap, in turn, is attached to my pram. I cannot say that I recall the pram itself with equal precision, though the buckle is part of the apparatus which keeps me there. But this small, almost irrelevant object swimming in the blurred circle of infant vision is extraordinarily vivid. I also remember the cold, acrid, metallic taste when I put the buckle in my mouth and sucked it.

My belief is that anyone who tries to remember his earliest childhood—the years before five—will come up with some detail or details rather like this one. What we call our 'earliest memories' are usually a mixture of two things. First, what we have been told about ourselves as small children. Our infant sayings and doings, recounted to us by parents and others, become part of our personal mythology, and this soon takes the place of true recollection. These external glimpses of ourselves are really nothing to do with the interior life or the true feelings and vision of infancy.

Our second way of remembering childhood is to think of those things which remained familiar to us for quite a long period; we tend to project what we recall about a slightly later stage in our lives backward into that dim area of time when we were living beings, but had no conscious knowledge of what we were. Interspersed among these two kinds of distorted recollection are the rare genuine ones.

The second kind of 'false' childhood memory has, of course, much greater validity than the first. I, who spent most of the first years of my life in one house, can of course claim to remember a good deal about it, even if I cannot always put a date to what I recall. Things coalesce around the buckle I have just described

—the thin leather strap to which it was attached, and then my pram. The pram sits on a patch of gravel outside a small and not at all beautiful tropical villa, with pebble-dash walls and a silvery roof of shingle. The villa is built on concrete piers; and, though it has only one storey, this is therefore raised about three feet above the ground. Beneath the building is a soft place of old leaves and bits of rubbish, chiefly paper and spiders' webs, and heaps of powdery dust. This forms a kind of symbolic no-man's-land or non-territory. Our lives hover above it without touching it; some of our dogs have puppies there which die, stifled in the dust.

The villa is edged on two sides by a verandah mantled in creeper, and floored with cracked red terrazzo. Ants hurry in and out of the cracks on their own mysterious errands. Beyond the verandah and within the house are dim rooms reached by full-length doors. The floors of these rooms are made of wide boards; partly covering the boards are worn straw mats which make a different texture to the naked soles of the feet and pressed against the walls of the rooms are occasional pieces of heavy furniture in the blackest tropical mahogany. In this country, where little is old, these mahogany pieces, which belonged to my grandfather, seem immensely antiquated.

The two rooms I am now thinking of form the family living-room and dining-room. The living-room is seldom used, since the verandah is much cooler and airier. It is, in fact, the tropical equivalent of a parlour or 'best room', a shrine to assorted family gods. One table, for instance, has a load of objects made of brass, conspicuous among them a couple of shell-cases picked up by my father on the battlefields of the First World War, and clustering round these are lesser talismans such as old horse-brasses and small oriental brass trays. On another, and smaller, table is a galaxy of little objects in silver: snuff-boxes, pill-boxes, and even a tiny silver chair. These are often polished; the tropical humidity makes them tarnish. The incised lines of the decoration are therefore choked with whitish powder, the dried remains of polish. Another perfectly focused memory is of the taste of this powder, which I would carefully pick out with a finger-nail, and put on the tip of my tongue. The flavour was not pleasant, but it somehow gave a sensual shock of surprise.

Leading off these two main rooms are the bedrooms of the house. To the right, across a narrow passage, is my parents' room. The passageway itself, which seems to serve no useful purpose, is a depository for an assortment of objects. On the wall is a rack with riding-whips, shooting-sticks, and dog-leads, and field glasses in their leather cases. There is also a bookcase full of decaying books, among them a full set of Kipling's works printed on India paper and bound in limp leather. These have suffered considerably, but not as much as another set—this time of the complete works of Jane Austen—from the effects of damp and silver-fish. The passageway derives from its contents a smell of old glue and mildewed paper.

My parents' bedroom is at the front of the house, and behind it is my father's dressing-room. As it happens, I can recall this in much greater detail than the bedroom itself. Like all the rooms not sheltered by the verandah, it has sash windows filled with panes of whitish frosted glass. These seem to make very definite the separation between 'inside' and 'outside' the house. When the upper sash is down, the bright blue square thus revealed seems incongruous. Beside the window are curtains of cheap cotton, very faded, which stretch only as far as the sill. They are never closed, but serve as a mute concession to domestic taste.

The principal piece of furniture in the dressing-room is a large and clumsy roll-top desk, and on this desk is an ancient type-writer whose keys seem very stiff to a child's fingers. One feature of this typewriter which particularly fascinates me, as soon as I am allowed to touch the machine, is the fact that the type has to be raised in a semi-circular fan before the keys are ready for operation. The desk is usually untidy, with bundles of letters and papers; the writing surface is also scattered with rusted paper-clips, and with perished rubber bands, ready to snap at a touch. This makes a contrast with the rest of the room, for, with this sole exception, my father is a man who is meticulous about his possessions, just as he is about his appearance. There is a rack of highly polished riding boots, and there are cupboards full of silk handkerchiefs, and matching dotted silk ties. This room, like the passage, has its own characteristic smell: a sour-sweet reek of Virginia tobacco, embrocation, and sweat.

On the other side of the house, to the right of the dining-room, lies the room which is used as my nursery. Strangely enough, I recall even less about this than about my parents' bedroom. It is a non-place, and my associations are those of fretfulness and bore-dom. In this room I was made to 'rest' for three interminable hours every afternoon; I lay on my cot with limbs braced and mind clenched against the outrage of this captivity.

But suddenly another perfectly formed memory discloses itself. The cot in which I was put resembled a cage, with high barred sides. The cage could be opened by undoing two little bolts whereupon one of the long sides fell outward and down-ward on hinges. Certainly I must have been very small, because it was still assumed that these two bolts would baffle me. So, for a time, they did, until one afternoon I succeeded in undoing them. Holding on to the top rail as it dropped, I was flung forward on to my two front teeth. The great jolt of pain was, I suspect, my first real experience of the world's capacity to inflict it. That the jolt had indeed been severe was proven later, when the time came for me to lose my milk teeth. The two which had taken the force of the fall turned out to have no roots, and slipped from the gum with apologetic ease. One of the replacements grew with a flaw in the enamel which shows to this day.

Behind the dining-room lay another verandah, part of which was surrounded by a wooden lattice (another cage), built so that my nurse and I could sleep there during the hottest part of the summer. I remember her undressing in the dark, long after I had gone to bed, with mysterious rustlings of blouse and underclothes.

The rest of this back verandah was the beginning of the ser-vants' territory. Out of it led the kitchen, the scullery and the pantry, in a line projecting at right angles from the rest of the house. Facing these rooms across the back yard, but detached from the rest of the house, were the servants' sleeping quarters —a row of poky little rooms, each with its own set of steps, but sheltered under a single continuous roof. The back verandah had a view not only of these, but of a kind of parody of them in miniature—a line of ramshackle chicken coops within an en-closure of wire mesh.

It is perhaps a little illogical to have spoken first about the house

and only now about the garden in which my pram—the pram
with which we began—was sitting. The area in which we lived
was suburban. There were many small villas, none beautiful,
none identical to any of the others—an endless set of permuta-
tions on the theme of architectural mediocrity. Each of these
villas was detached from the others, and set back from the road
in its own plot. As land had not been specially valuable when
they were built, these plots were often quite large, at least in
terms of a child's geography.

The gardens were always divided into two roughly equal
areas; what Jamaicans still describe as the front yard and the back.
The front yard was strictly for show. Ours was bordered with a
hedge of poinsettias, which bloomed in the Christmas season, and
standing sentinel at either corner were two flame-of-the-forest, or
poinciana, trees. As a child I always associated these two trees
with the kind elephants in story books, because their limbs had
the sinuosity of an elephant's trunk, and their bark resembled
smooth grey hide. The poincianas seeded themselves by means of
vast pods, like outsize wooden models of ordinary runner beans.
Occasionally these pods served as bats in desultory games of
cricket, with a pebble for the ball.

Two other trees grew in the front garden: a small frangipani, at
its most characteristic when leafless and covered in large waxy
cream-and-golden flowers, looking as if someone had rather un-
skilfully modelled a tree out of twigs and wax. And in the middle
of the lawn grew a lignum-vitae. It seems hard to conjure up any
texture or image where this latter is concerned; simply, I believe,
because it was a favourite topic of conversation with adults.
When I try to recall what it looked like, I hear a hearty adult voice
pronouncing the words: 'the hardest wood in the world, you
know', and what flashes on to the screen of the retina is a clumsily
carved ashtray made by some local craftsman, or a set of coasters
from a tourist shop.

The main glories of the front yard—at least in intention—were
the lawn and the surrounding flowerbeds. The lawn varied from
green to brown according to the state of the local water supply,
and also according to the degree of industry, or the lack of it, with
which the current garden-boy had pushed our heavy lawn-mower

across it. It looked its best when pearled with the silvery drops of the water-sprinkler, spinning two arcs of water away from itself, while a small dog cavorted round, barking at the motion.

The flowerbeds which surrounded the lawn and edged the gravel drive were filled with an incongruous mixture of plants. There were gaudy tropical shrubs, with variegated leaves, which looked like the product of mad craftswomen working in leather; there were jasmine bushes alive with bee-humming birds, which darted about the sweetly scented flowers like drops of molten metal; there were sickly English petunias, and sicklier roses, garish zinnias, and the great raw-meat-coloured blossoms of the canna lilies.

As I describe the front yard there surges up within me awful desolating boredom which I used to feel when turned out to play in it, or (as people said) 'to get some fresh air'. I only had to set foot in it to be overcome by a desire to be anywhere but where I was. The sole pastime of my early childhood which spontaneously took place in the front yard was one which made use of the deep ditches which surrounded each flowerbed. One could build mud dams in these, which turned them into miniature canals. Then armadas of matchboxes and flotillas of paper boats could be set adrift upon the soupy water. The listless motion echoed my own listlessness as I played with them.

The back yard was a different matter—a place of weeds and stones and sheds and washhouses and the enclosure for chickens already described. Through it rang the loud voices of the servants, and in one corner flickered the bonfire on which my father's bath water was heated in a square jerry can.

This bonfire always fascinated me. I would sit beside it, gazing into fiery caverns within it, while the heat of the flames fanned my face as I bent nearer and nearer. From the fire and the twisted shapes of the charred sticks I made new creatures to inhabit my imagination.

Imagination: this was the dimension which lay beyond the realities which I've been describing. My life as a small child was a series of immensely elaborate fantasies, nourished perhaps by the fact that I was an only child and much alone. I was always both disappointed by and impatient with the apparent inability of adults to enter into these fantasies, or even to understand what was being asked of them. The various rooms of the house, the front yard, and especially the back, were the theatres for a series of elaborate solitary games. All kinds of objects made up for the lack of company: toy cars and lead soldiers, and costume jewellery rifled from my mother's boxes. Books pulled from the bookcases were used to build many-storied Aztec palaces on the nursery floor—these structures were furnished and decorated with beads, and inhabited by miniature guardsmen in scarlet coats. Or sometimes the lead soldiers would be deployed on the bare boards of my father's dressing-room, or on a hilly terrain made from more books, now draped in the green baize cloth from the card-table.

What I liked best were games with some element of destruction: the Aztec palaces would be shaken by earthquakes, the soldiers shot down in their ranks with a toy cannon. The fire on which my father's bath water was heated was, however, essential for the destructive game that I most enjoyed.

Fire frightened as well as fascinated me. Throughout my childhood, for example, I refused even to strike a match. Yet, when the heavy can of water was taken off its little fire I always asked for the fire itself to be left. Sometimes I merely roasted potatoes and green bananas cadged from the cook. More often I engineered the destruction of men and buildings, the fall of Babylon, a city which I became minuscule to inhabit. Toy forts went up in flames; heroic soldiers stood at their posts till the fire took them, and the silvery lead ran down into the ashes and embers, to be found afterwards, when the fire had died, twisted into new and bizarre shapes. Later I developed a new variant of this game: a covey of toy boats jigged on the choppy waves of a galvanized tin washtub full of water, each of them aflame and burning to the waterline, with caps from a cap-pistol concealed in their cargo to provide sudden explosions and jets of fire.

Such games could fill a whole day, but other days were dull and flat, and I sickened of my own company, and mooned about the flowerbeds, digging my nails into the leathery leaves of the shrubs, to see the white sap well out of them like alien blood.

CHAPTER TWO

MY CHILDHOOD WORLD was, however, inhabited by existences other than my own; and these existences were as much animals as people. In case the statement seems obscure, I ought to explain that not only did animals seem to me to be people, but that I also tended to be strongly conscious of human beings in their animal aspects; their various smells, for instance.

More even than is the case with most houses where there are children, ours was a menagerie. There were never fewer than three dogs, and to these should be added the denizens of an aquarium, a cage full of budgerigars, various stray cats, and the poultry pecking the packed dirt of the back yard. Other fauna included the ants sauntering from the cracks in the verandah, the humming-birds busy at the jasmine bushes, and innumerable flying insects. Add to these such other visitants as the huge spiders we sometimes found trapped in the bath, their long legs thrashing in vain against the steep white enamel sides, and the total of livestock grows even larger.

The dogs were very different from one another, both in aspect and in character. The first I can recall are an old scottie, paralysed in her hind legs, and a deaf white bull terrier bitch, who was famous for her savagery. The latter was often left tied up in the hot sun of the back yard, where I skirted round her, calf-muscles trembling, while she growled in a continuous rumble. But one of these dogs soon died, and the other was put down.

The current dogs, during the middle stretch of my childhood, were a fat, good-natured dachshund called Sally, a hysterical cross-bred terrier named Tessa, and assorted mongrels. The most memorable of the mongrels were mother and son. Though so closely related, they could not have been a greater contrast in character. The mother was sly and foxy: she had no name because she never answered to one. The son had none of her brains, but was a large good-natured canine half-wit. I called him Jumble, after William's dog in the 'Just William' stories by Richmal Crompton, which I then adored, but the servants soon corrupted this to Jumbo, and Jumbo he remained. In particular, he had huge feet, and no sense of where and where not to put them.

These assorted dogs, being left, and in that favourable climate, so much to their own devices, developed a kind of tribal organization which was not very different from the packs formed by their remote ancestors. Into this tribe I was admitted. Delicately, they would groom the skin of my bare legs, from the bottom edge of my shorts downwards, tickling the skin caressingly with their teeth, in a way which made all the little hairs stand up. Then they would turn and groom one another in the same fashion. Like me, these dogs played elaborate games—some innocently high spirited, some less innocent.

One afternoon, for instance, at the time of the siesta, when I had somehow or other escaped from my ritual incarceration in the nursery, I sat alone on the back verandah, watching the dogs, who were busy at the side of the hen run. Soon I got up and walked closer, in order to see more. There, where the weeds and the cow parsley shook persistently, I found the dachshund digging away at the earth at the bottom of the wire with her powerful forepaws. The other three dogs stood watching her, backs rigid, tails stiff and quivering, but made no attempt to help. One looked up and caught my eye, but seemed to sense that I would do nothing.

After fifteen minutes or so of vigorous excavation, the dachshund had made a tunnel large enough to allow first herself, and then the others, to squeeze under the fence. For a moment they all stood stock-still, while the hens crowded to the opposite corner of the run, cackling uneasily. Then the dogs exploded into movement, and the massacre began. The swift terrier and the two mongrels drove the quarry for the dachshund to snap at with her long jaws. The air was filled with an increasing cloud of feathers. Some of the hens made their escape and roosted out of reach in the branches of a small tree, swearing angrily at their persecutors. Others were trapped and mangled. Eventually the racket was such that the cook, roused at last from her afternoon sleep, came to see what was going on. My parents ate roast chicken for several nights thereafter.

My reluctance to intervene sprang, I think, from several causes, chief among them the usual childhood pleasure in mischief and disaster. But there was also my feeling of loyalty towards the dogs, creatures whom I believed I understood, and whom I thought might probably understand me. But lastly there was the fact that, throughout my early childhood, I disliked chickens with an almost obsessional dislike, for which I can give no explanation. It is true, of course, that the chickens of the tropics tend to be particularly unattractive: drab, dishevelled and mean of eye. Some of those we kept were of the species known locally as 'peel-neck chicken', with a bare, raw-looking neck like that of a vulture.

If the chickens were our dogs' predestined victims, the parrot who lived in the thick honeysuckle vine that shrouded the verandah was their determined and highly successful tormentor. I have never believed in the supposed stupidity of parrots since my acquaintanceship with this bird. He refused to learn the inane phrases which we occasionally tried to teach him, but eavesdropped on the whole household, and put what he learned to good use. For instance, he could imitate me to perfection—a demanding, childish voice, calling determinedly for nurse or mother. Later, he elaborated a long imitation which was like a sketch by an old-fashioned music hall comedian. The victim was my mother, as she gossiped on the telephone: 'Hello! Oh, it's you, dear? Yes—yes—yes. Blahblahblahblah.' The open English vowels were skilfully parodied.

The parrot's most successful 'turn', however, was an act of aggression directed at the dogs, whom he never lost a chance to discomfit. From within that stubby red and green body, regularly at five in the afternoon, there would emerge an alarming mechanical rattle. It was just the time when my father was due home from the office, and, to the dogs, the sound the parrot made was evidently the exact equivalent of the sound which his old Plymouth sedan made as it laboured along the road. On hearing this deceptive rattle the whole tribe of dogs would at once rush to the front gate, barking joyfully. The parrot, a master of ventri-

loquism as well as of mimicry, would lead the pack, by means of
gradual crescendos and decrescendos of noise, along the gravel
and right up to the front steps. Then would come the sound of
the car door being opened and then slammed again. The dogs,
by this time frantic, unable to believe the conflicting evidence of
their divided senses, would leap and bound about the spot where
my father might now be supposed to stand. Finally, there came
the climax of the imitation: my father's voice scolding the poor
beasts for their unruliness. Vanquished, and overcome with guilt
and amazement in equal proportions, the dogs would slink away
with their tails between their legs.

After each of these triumphantly malicious performances, the
parrot would emerge from the depths of the creeper within
which he had hidden himself, and swing upon a stem in par-
oxysms of near-human laughter. The only thing which seemed to
give him more pleasure than the unfailing success of this decep-
tion was a good, solid downpour of rain. Then, too, he would
come out of the creeper, and plant himself upon a springy stem,
bouncing and swaying as the water drenched his feathers, and
shrieking for joy at every lightning flash and clap of thunder.

Besides being the tormentor of the dogs, the parrot was also
the furtive enemy of the fish which I kept in an aquarium on the
table in the corner of the verandah. In any case, these fish showed
a susceptibility to mysterious diseases, and would often be discovered in the morning, floating swollen and belly upward on
the surface of the viscid water which even the most frequent
scourings could never keep clear and clean. Neon Tetras, Glass-
fish, Black Mollies—all duly perished within a week or two of
purchase. Two species were hardier—the common guppy,
fished with the help of a jam jar from the lily pond in the botanical gardens, and the magnificent Siamese Fighting Fish. I had
several of these creatures in succession. Too fierce to be kept with
other species, or with one another, each reigned in turn over a
tank arranged for his sole convenience. To see the fish in his full
glory, one brought a small mirror up to the glass, or lowered it
into the tank. Suddenly catching sight of what he took to be a
rival, the Fighting Fish would spread his red and purple fins. His
whole body then seemed to swell, and he darted savagely towards

the mirror image, shrinking back again as his snout felt the cold shock of the glass.

These fish were hardy as well as fierce, and for a long time we could not make out why they regularly vanished from the tank, leaving not a trace behind them. At first we supposed that they had leapt out, to perish on the floor, though no search ever revealed a body. But at last, one day, the parrot was discovered perched on the very rim of the tank, and his guilt seemed established. Nevertheless, he remained the monarch of the creeper, attentive only to my mother's blandishments, fiercely suspicious of the rest of the household, and always ready to administer a sly nip if one came too near.

The parrot's own end was sad. He caught a cold, which turned into pneumonia. He withdrew into his cage. Though he scarcely ever used this, the door was always left open. Now the bars between himself and the world seemed to give him some kind of comfort and protection. He sat on his perch, feathers fluffed out, looking like a worn-out feather duster. My mother coaxed him on to her finger every couple of hours in order to force a few drops of whisky down his throat. For a moment, this would revive him. But in the end it was no good; he died within a few days. It was a kind of tribute to his stubborn individualism that we never had the heart to get another parrot, though other animals were usually replaced.

In fact, the tropics were cruel to our pets. They died off almost as rapidly as the first colonists had died in the days of the yellow fever. Distemper took the dogs—those that were not run over by Jamaica's reckless drivers; the fish died as I have described; the budgerigars developed underwing swellings, or were found lying stark and dead on the floor of their aviary, having perished in the night of an epileptic seizure.

Besides their vulnerability, it seems to me that there was always something wilder and more independent about our animals than there would have been about the pets of an English household. The climate set them freer to range outside; the doors of the house, the gate into the garden were alike never shut. More than this, the fierceness of the tropics entered their spirits. If I think now of my childhood, one image that persistently comes to mind is of myself lying awake at night in a hot and rumpled bed. The moonlight is blazing through the frosted glass of the bedroom window, and I know that outside the trees will be throwing inky shadows on the moon-bleached grass of the lawn, and that the moon will have turned the meat-coloured blooms of the Cannas to a sinister purplish black. There is a tingling noise of frogs and insects, a chirring and chirping just on the limits of hearing, and then, far off, a dog howls, and then another, and another, and another, the howling gradually swelling in volume and coming nearer until it is right outside the window.

Once or twice, unable to sleep, I raised the bedroom sash and saw mysterious comings and goings, as if a whole conclave of the dogs of the neighbourhood had assembled. I used to imagine that they had a social life of their own in the night-time, which was nothing to do with the social life of their masters, but which was just as elaborately structured.

For a brief time, the household sheltered an animal which seemed to symbolize and sum up all this animal wildness: a young tom cat with yellow eyes, the son of a pregnant stray cat who one day decided that we were to look after her and feed her and provide a place for the impending birth. She had her kittens in the dark cupboard at the end of the bedroom passage. Five of them were ordinary grey-striped creatures like herself. The sixth, much larger than the rest even at birth, was the white tom. From the start his mother favoured him; he was always first at the teat. When the kittens became more active, and began to stir from her side, tumbling over the edges of the shallow wooden box with which we had provided her, it was always the white one that the mother looked for first. Seizing him by the scruff, she carefully returned him to the nest, and only then set off in search of the others.

The white kitten grew amazingly. Soon he was twice as large as his siblings. Arrogant, fierce, untrustworthy, untameable, he savaged hands and cheeks, climbed every tree in the garden in search of birds' nests, and never cried to be rescued. He stalked the lizards on the paths, and often caught them despite their lightning quickness. One of his feats—though it was not, I think, an act of calculated malice such as the parrot would have perpetrated—was to catch a mouse (which may have been his first) and to bring it proudly, quaking and wounded as it was, into the midst of one of my mother's cocktail parties. Then, after about two years of uneasy co-existence with the rest of the household, the white tom disappeared. I should not be surprised to hear that there was now a race of savage snow-white cats wandering in the rain-forests of Jamaica.

These were the beasts to which we could claim some kind of ownership: ownership which they acknowledged or not as it suited them. The island teemed with other animal life, and the sea around it still more so. Much of this had a rather baleful beauty, though the one really deadly creature, the fer-de-lance snake, had been killed off years before by mongooses imported from India to do the job. These latter, surviving, had bred and multiplied, and now satisfied themselves with unwary chickens in country parishes. But, even in the suburbs of Kingston, the creatures were always stirring. In our garden, praying mantises stalked the stems of the fading roses with a disdainful air. Put a pair of these in a jam jar, and one of them would immediately try to decapitate the other with her saw-toothed fore-arms. Scorpions lurked occasionally between the sheets or in one's shoes; centipedes scuttled across the terrazzo of the front verandah, and on its supporting pillars little lizards waited, each with an orange sac pulsing under his chin to attract the flies. Leaning over the dock railings at Kingston harbour, one might hope to see a jelly fish opening and closing like a mad umbrella in the clear water, six feet below. As one swam from the beaches, little fish, their spines and stomachs visible through the transparent flesh, came and nibbled at one's legs, in the hope that one was a piece of carrion. John-crows perpetually soared overhead, on the lookout for dead meat.

Carrion itself soon swarmed with new life. A dead cat in the roadway shimmered within moments with an armour of flies; a grasshopper was quickly hollowed out by ants, each trekking away with a morsel of flesh in his jaws. Often one saw stirring in the pathway the wings of a dead butterfly, already severed from the body, and moving in different directions as the scavengers carried them away.

CHAPTER THREE

WHEN I TRY to picture myself as a small child, I seldom think of myself in the presence of my parents. It is the animals I remember—and, of course, the servants. Despite the fact that my father was an impoverished colonial civil servant, the small house was full of servants—a cook, a parlour-maid, various cleaning women and laundresses who came and went as occasion required. For much of the time, the most central person in my existence was my nurse. She meant so much to me that my memories of her are always a little out of focus, like an object held too close to the eye.

She was a Jamaican—handsome, well-educated, self-possessed, never out of temper except when engaged in debate with the other servants, who resented her status in the household. She seldom raised her voice (in a country where voices are always raised) and seemed to detach herself both from the world of white people—though she was light-complexioned—and from that of the Jamaican country parishes where she had been brought up. She was reluctant, even, to talk about her own life before she came to us. The one story I can ever remember her telling me was about a mischievous trick which she and her cronies had sometimes played when she was a schoolgirl. They would carefully save pieces of broken glass and crockery, and then, when a specially dark night came, one of them would lie down in the road which led from the village rum-shop, and the others would outline her limbs with these hoarded fragments, then the model would be lifted up by arms and legs to leave the outline intact. The drunkards, stumbling home by lanternlight, much later in the evening, were confronted by what they took to be an apparition: the glimmering fragments of porcelain seemed to them like the much-feared duppy, or malignant ghost, of Jamaican folklore. With despairing yells, they would run away.

Having told this tale, my nurse seemed to regret it. She would never tell me more. She brought me up to think 'white'; I was admonished not to have a Jamaican accent, I was subtly made aware of the difference between myself and the coloured children playing outside in the roadway. My untainted speech and staid good manners were much admired by my mother's friends as I handed round the nuts and savouries, or brought fresh drinks at cocktail parties.

The other servants are present in my mind with much greater clarity; they formed a whole tribe or society, with its internal feuds, its quarrels and alliances, but always with a basic loyalty between its members. One was never more aware of this than when they lined up weekly to be paid, taking the little piles of notes and silver from in front of my mother on the dining-room table: so much for wages, and so much extra for food, which they bought and cooked for themselves. The differences in diet was also one of the most salient marks of the difference between 'them' and 'us'. I often ventured into the kitchen to ask for a taste of the little starchy messes that sat cooking on a charcoal brazier—this alien diet was the only one I liked.

The dominant personality among the servants was our fat cook Elma, who was to stay with us until we finally left Jamaica for good. Loud of voice, occasionally bad-tempered, she seemed to fill the little kitchen with her buxomness. Nita, the parlourmaid, was totally, almost comically, different—a thin, twig-like being, the blackness of whose face was ornamented with a pair of gold-rimmed spectacles. She was usually as quiet as Elma was noisy, and when the two of them quarrelled, as they often did, Nita would retire into sulky silences and little whining replies to direct questions. She moved around the house like a shadow. Much of her time was spent in picking up my discarded clothes, and in restoring scattered toys to their places. I never thought of tidying up, and indeed was never asked to.

These three, the nurse, the cook and the parlourmaid, were the senior members of the household hierarchy—except that the nurse ceded her place, holding herself apart, scarcely seeming to acknowledge that she was a servant at all. This left Elma in charge of the household—always ready to lay an extra place at table if a guest arrived unexpectedly, apparently unflustered when, having asked for dinner at eight, my parents returned late from some cocktail party, and did not present themselves till nine. Elma was well aware of her own skills in this respect, and did not like to have her methods challenged. If my mother happened to query some detail, the cook would retreat into a torrent of dialect explanations. This defence was always effective, as my mother had not been born in the island and had great difficulty in understanding the local patois, especially when spoken both copiously and rapidly.

Elma bossed the casual labour who in turn did the rough work. There was, for example, Mary, who came occasionally to scrub floors and help with the laundry—Mary, with tight plaits, a great gap-toothed smile, and a forehead always beaded with pearls of sweat. Wherever she was, indoors amid the rolled-up mats or outside bending over a tin wash-tub, a gaggle of children followed her around. These children were all Mary's, but after a very Jamaican fashion, being by different fathers and without benefit of matrimony. Mary, in fact, was just at the beginning of the arduous career which might eventually produce a Jamaican matriarch—the authoritative head of a whole tribe of descendants, daughters and daughters' daughters, past work perhaps, but supported and respected by them all.

Sophie, the cook whom my mother had employed when she first came to the island, was just such a matriarch. Now retired, she still came to see us on public holidays and at Christmas. A thin, vigorous old woman, she wore the traditional market woman's bandana, and puffed at a clay pipe with a contented air. There was already a certain contrast between Sophie and her successor Elma, who was a generation younger: Sophie still had a country air, which Elma lacked; though Elma was burly and vigorous, it was Sophie who seemed earthy, close to the soil.

Nevertheless, some remnants of old customs survived. The back yard and kitchen-quarters of our little villa swarmed with visitors—vendors, passers-by, the servants' relations from country parts. Early in the morning, one would hear Elma's voice upraised as she haggled with an itinerant pedlar of oysters or black crabs, delicacies needed for the dinner-party my mother was giving that night. These visitors were seldom discouraged by the fact that the dogs detested them and ran out with barks and growls to greet each new arrival.

As dusk fell, all the servants but my nurse, and any casual callers who might be present, gathered on the back verandah to listen while one of their number read aloud, in a laborious sing-song, from the day's newspaper. These gatherings, too, were a reminder of how things were done in the villages up-country, where the story-teller sat under a paraffin lamp outside the rum-shop and related old tales, or spun new ones from the day's gossip. The living-in servants, and not merely my nurse, were perhaps proud on occasion that they had cut themselves off from the old ways, and were no longer country people. But there still remained a bond between them and those whom they regarded as mere peasants; the current of island life swirled and eddied boisterously even here, in the white-dominated middle-class suburbs of Kingston.

The individual who was most frequently in conflict with the tone of the district, the well-conducted rhythm of the household, was the garden-boy—whoever he might happen to be at the time. The other servants remained with us: the garden-boy was a mutable factor, the rebellious male in our little community of servants, liable at any moment to be fired for idleness or insolence, always at odds with my father, always liable to provoke Elma's or the nurse's wrath. Each successive garden-boy was lazier and less willing than his predecessor. True enough, some of the duties assigned to these strapping young men were bizarre. When the war came, and petrol was very short, it was the current garden-boy who was assigned to take me to kindergarten—I riding my tricycle, he weaving behind me on a bicycle, holding a Japanese paper sunshade above my head. But I do not remember that this apparently humiliating task was responsible for an explosion. The garden-boy of the day and I rather enjoyed our little outings and saw nothing ridiculous about them—it was, after all, a place where and a moment when people were sawing up saloon cars in order to turn them into horse-drawn buggies. Our little pro-cession to school was part of the expedients and ingenuities of wartime. Indeed, my impression is that the paper sunshade was a touch that the garden-boy may have insisted on adding for himself.

Of course, it would not do to pretend that conditions in pre-war Jamaica were idyllic; that racial friction never existed, or at least was hidden from the awareness of a child. In 1938, when I was five, there were serious riots in Kingston. My father was summoned back from leave in England to help to deal with the emergency. The world of black people hovered always at the edge of awareness, as something very different from, and alien to, the world which we ourselves moved in.

This mysteriously different society made its impact on the consciousness in sharply different and indeed contradictory ways. At Christmas-time, for instance, there was the long row of booths along East Parade in downtown Kingston. I can just remember being taken to see them, at night one year, at some hour long past my usual bedtime, and gazing at them from a distance, thronged with customers, piled with cheap toys in tin and wood and plastic, festooned with candy-floss and bunches of balloons, the whole garishly lit with acetylene flares. I was not allowed to stop and look closely, as I longed to do, and wondered why.

A number of other crowd-scenes also linger in the mind's eye. Particularly vivid is a Catholic church fête, perhaps at Easter, to which my nurse once took me. Here, once again, there were booths, selling not toys but home-made cakes and sweets, and assorted jumble. One stall especially fascinated me: it sold plaster saints. My nurse, seeing how my eyes fastened on them, bought me a white plaster relief of the Virgin, her body backed by a burst of sun-rays, and the whole sprinkled with little flecks of gold dust. For a long time I thought it was the most beautiful object I had ever seen, and it stood on top of the nursery cupboard, where I could see it last thing at night. Since we were garrison-church Protestant, and not very frequent church-goers at that, its religious significance quite escaped me: I liked it for what it was.

Despite my fascination with the plaster saints, there was another aspect of this fête which also obsessed and troubled me, though it took me a long time to identify it. As I remembered the look, the smell, the taste of the event—such things rolled round and round in my mind for weeks or even months—it occurred to me how few white faces there had been. Those that were present belonged to the priests. The rest of the crowd, decorous, neatly dressed in clothes which I already recognized as middle-class, were black people and brown people. This puzzled me: it seemed to contradict an order of affairs which I thought of as firmly established. And then, too, the home-made sweets had tasted different from the sweets I was accustomed to: they were grainier, more powerfully flavoured with coconut and vanilla; above all they were *sweeter*, with the powerful sweetness of raw sugar-cane. This, too, had to be added to the list of significant differences, of things I didn't understand.

Mostly, however, this other society manifested itself in ways which could be accepted without puzzlement. Driving out into the countryside on Sunday mornings, we would suddenly meet great flocks of black people on foot, most of them dressed in starched immaculate white, though some of the younger ones wore a shade of blazing sugar-almond pink, a colour which my parents and their friends could still, without self-consciousness, refer to as 'nigger pink'. These people were, I was told, going to church, and indeed later on we would pass little tin-roofed chapels whose walls seemed to bulge with the fervour of singing. Or else, as we approached, we would hear a little bell clanking wildly and discordantly, as the congregation pushed to get inside the building, and hear what the preacher had to say to them.

Other signs of religious belief were occasionally to be found planted by the roadside, especially in what were described as 'bad areas', or in the remoter country parts. A little hut, placed on a ridge above a gulley, would have, fluttering beside it, a ragged blue flag on a tall pole—the sign, I was told, of an obeah cultist. Obeah was the Jamaican version of voodoo, the remnants of the dark religion which had been brought with them from Africa by the slaves. Its doctrines concerned spells and possession by spirits. Despite the fact that it was forbidden by law, and the further fact that the prohibition was enforced by frequent prosecutions, one often encountered evidence of the existence of obeah beliefs, and sometimes, indeed, met with declared practitioners.

Later, when I was at school, the building was occasionally frequented by the local obeah-man. I think he came to exact tribute, in cash or kind, from the maids in their quarters at the back, but, if he had been given a glass or two of white rum by his hostesses, the mood would take him to look in on us in our classrooms, which had french doors which stood open to the loggias and balconies with which the building was surrounded. He was a middle-aged man, slightly bent in the shoulders, but very muscular, dressed in a kind of jester's uniform of fluttering rags and tatters, with several ruined shirts worn one over another. In his hand he carried a little wooden club, slightly curved, so that it had almost the shape of a boomerang. This club was painted the chalky obeah blue, and under the blue was another layer of white paint. Various cabbalistic signs were scratched through the blue layer, so that they appeared in white, but, since the obeah-man would never in any circumstances surrender his baton of office, it was impossible to get a close look at what they were, or to decide what they might signify.

He would appear suddenly in the doorway, interrupting the lesson by rapping on the doorpost with his club. When every eye was turned towards him, he would intone his two ritual phrases (which never varied) in a deep, croaking voice: 'Be good, child-ren! Obey your master, child-ren.' Then he would laugh sardonically, turn on his heel, and lope away.

No comment was ever made by members of the teaching staff about these interruptions. The lesson would resume where it had halted. The inability of those in charge of us to find some formula wherein the witch-doctor could be contained was somehow symbolic of the fissures to be found within Jamaican society taken as a whole. But even in the suburbs of Kingston, even at home, one was conscious of this undertone of strangeness, like a sound on the very limit of hearing, like a soft African drum-beat accompanying a Czerny piano-exercise. Existence was made of two parts, which did not quite fit together as they were conventionally supposed to do.

Sometimes the night sounds of dogs and frogs and insects which I listened to so fretfully and wakefully, and often so fearfully, included another element, a subdued chanting, which seemed to float, if the wind was exactly in the right quarter, from the slums and shanty-towns on the other side of the city. What was it? The shouting of revivalist congregations? The outcries of obeah ceremonial? Nobody could tell me. It was the undertone made manifest and physically audible, a fact now, no longer a metaphor for a quality one could not otherwise define.

CHAPTER FOUR

IF I SPEAK last of all, in these early chapters, about my parents, and, through them, about the world that white people moved in, it is for a variety of reasons. The first is, quite simply, that when I try to picture myself as a small child, I seldom think of myself in my parents' presence.

My father was a colonial civil servant. Eventually he became Assistant Colonial Secretary: third man in the administrative hierarchy. He worked long hours, usually leaving the house in the morning before I was dressed, and often returning to it long after my bedtime. As soon as war broke out, my mother took a job with some voluntary organization, and was out of the house for half the day.

Nevertheless, despite my parents' frequent absences from the household, a number of rituals were preserved. My father's main interest, besides his job, was horses. He was a first-class polo-player, and strained his resources to keep a couple of polo-ponies and a groom. He was also a steward of the Jamaica Jockey Club. Family outings, therefore, tended to centre either upon the polo-ground or the racecourse.

Polo was played on Saturday afternoons. The polo-ground lay, appropriately enough, in the midst of the Liguanea racecourse —though this was no longer much used for racing. The ground was a dusty field surrounded by low boarding against which the wooden balls clanked resoundingly. Under the blazing afternoon sun, the fat but nimble polo-ponies wheeled and swooped, the riders shouting encouragement to one another. High up in the blue, silk-sack clouds were driven across the sky by the afternoon wind from the sea. From the drab grass little whirlwinds would suddenly arise, carrying scraps of paper and dead leaves twenty feet into the air, flinging particles of grit stingingly into the eyes. Outside the small wooden pavilion the polo-wives sat and gossiped, their knitting-needles clicking in a rhythm that seemed to echo the distant click of the polo-mallets. And around the women their children played, fighting, pulling one another's hair, becoming shriller and more bad-tempered as the long hot afternoon wore on.

At the end of each chukka, the players would canter back to change their mounts. Sometimes, in the interval between games, I would be lifted on to the back of a barrel-bellied polo-pony. To my father's disappointment, I was always afraid. My short legs could not grip the pony's sides properly, and his sweaty hide chafed the insides of my bare thighs, at the point where my shorts left off. I clutched the pommel of the saddle as the groom walked the beast up and down, and soon begged to get off.

Sometimes, on windy days, I would be allowed to bring my kite with me in the back of the car. This meant that I could wander off, away from the noise and bustle round the pavilion, and slowly coax the frail bamboo-and-tissue-paper contraption into the air. Quite suddenly, the breeze would take it, and it would dart impetuously upward, its tail lashing. The wind blew so steadily that there was not much to do once the kite was properly launched—it leant into the wind, and the string hummed against one's fingers, for as long as one cared to stand there and act as the anchor which prevented its escape.

After the game, the grown-ups had their ritual hour of conviviality in the pavilion, which children were never allowed to enter. By this time the brief tropical dusk was already fading, and a little group of us sat disconsolate on the wooden step, too tired now even to fight. From the building there drifted a powerful smell of sweat, cigarette smoke and alcohol, and a great indistinguishable roar of adult talk. Soon, but never soon enough for me, it would be time to find our way back to the old Plymouth sedan, and I would curl up in the back seat with the dogs, thankful that another Sunday afternoon was over.

Race-meetings were something I much preferred to these never-ending hours at the polo-field. I liked the noise and colour of the crowd. More, I was interested in the racing itself, because I was a gambler. My father used to give me sixpence if I guessed the name of one of the horses in the first three. Afterwards, he even increased the allowance to a shilling if I was able to spot the winner. This system must have cost him a good many shillings and sixpences, as I was gifted with uncanny foresight—or, at least, we went to the races so often that my knowledge of form became professionally expert. If my mother and her friends had habitually taken the tips which I handed out with juvenile lordliness, they would have tended to finish the afternoon's racing richer than in fact they did.

Jamaican racing had a certain rough-and-readiness which occasionally became outright violence. I remember with some vividness the riot which followed the stewards' disqualification of a fancied mare in a big race. Her angry Syrian owners immediately rushed the stewards' box, which was a kind of gazebo raised on stilts beside the winning post. A confused mêlée took place. My father, who was short, was soon knocked to the floor, and had his monocle smashed. He said cheerfully, later, that, since he could see nothing, he had remained where he was on the boards, lashing out at any stomach which happened to loom above him.

The briskly gregarious social life led by my parents and their friends also extended to their children. We, too, were always being thrust into one another's company—at the Cubs, at one another's birthday parties, on the beach, during summer holidays in the cool of the mountains. In my case, these encounters were not usually a success. I was not a child whom other children liked, and I did not on the whole like other children. Adults often refused to accept the passionate aversion which I felt for certain of my contemporaries, and which they, in turn, felt for me. For example, my parents had some rich friends with a splendid house a little further out of Kingston than ours was. These friends had three children: a boy of exactly my own age, and two little girls, one of them still in her pram. Donald's mother was constantly telephoning my mother, to ask her to let me come over for the afternoon. Tearfully I would plead to be let off, and my mother would make increasingly lame excuses on my behalf. The day always came, however, when it was impossible to postpone the visit any longer.

Usually it was the McPatricks' car and driver that came to

collect me. As soon as the car drew up, and the door opened, Donald and I would begin insulting one another. By the time we reached the nursery, we had already begun delivering blows. The afternoon was spent in endless, exhausting pursuits and ambushes. We chased each other round the garden, tripping, kicking, scuffling, hair-pulling. Nursery-tea, at which we both of us appeared tousled, out-of-breath and tear-streaked, provided only the briefest respite in an exhausting afternoon. On the whole Donald had much the advantage during our struggles—he was an astonishingly pretty child, an accomplished liar (any crime, such as making his sisters cry, could swiftly be blamed on me), and a wonderfully lithe and vicious fighter, willing to use teeth or nails if occasion offered. The only things that I could put in the scales against all this were, first of all, the fact that I was a guest —but Donald paid no attention to the fact—and, secondly, that desperation occasionally gave me strength and cunning. I once completely drenched him by luring him into the midst of the elaborate lawn-sprinkler system in the garden, and then turning the tap. Donald, who was a foppish child as well as a pretty one, was correspondingly upset. Even after this misdemeanour, his mother continued to pursue me with invitations.

Occasions which I especially dreaded were my own birthday parties. As the date approached, I would be increasingly filled with gloom. My mother would be busy with lists—people we had to 'pay back'. Sulkily I would demur at this name or that: 'I can't stand him', I would say; or 'You know we always fight'. Eventually the invitations would be agreed, and the day itself would arrive. The cars would arrive and deposit the little guests, a few accompanied by their nannies. Their mothers would return for them just in time for a quick sundowner. Meanwhile we were on our own—we eyed each other with flinty expressions, calculating how the lines of battle would be drawn up.

It must be admitted that there were indeed gatherings which were less thoroughly disastrous than my birthday-parties generally turned out to be. We were less likely to fall out with one another on expeditions, for instance, than we were at parties. One popular way of spending an afternoon was to go out to Rock Fort, on the shores of Kingston Harbour. There, beside the disused fortifications which dated from the eighteenth century, was a small, vaulted mineral bath. The tingling coolness of the water, which welled up from a hidden spring, was very different to swim in from the tepid stickiness of the sea itself. And of course we all swam well; we leapt into the pool like so many little frogs, and set the reflections eddying on the whitewashed walls.

Another expedition—not very frequent because it called for a great deal of organizing—was a boat trip across Kingston Harbour, and out into the open sea, to visit some coral islets that lay just beyond the harbour mouth. We would all of us crowd into a fat old tub of a launch at the yacht-club jetty, great baskets of food and drink would be handed down to us, and after ten minutes' anxious fussing with a balky engine the mooring rope would be cast off, and we would be away across the harbour, with our wake curving away behind us.

Kingston Harbour is an enormous expanse of perfectly calm water, almost landlocked, with the long thin promontory of the Palisadoes curving out like an arm to protect it from the violence of the open sea. At the very tip of the promontory lay the remains of the pirate town of Port Royal, once the headquarters of Sir Henry Morgan, and later destroyed in a great seventeenth-century earthquake.

On either side, but especially on the more sheltered shore which faced inward, the promontory was fringed with mangrove swamps. The pungent smell of the mangroves, strange plants which raised themselves on unlovely and knobbly legs above the water, came drifting out to us, as we puttered along in the channel which drew gradually closer to the Palisadoes as it came nearer to the harbour entrance. This channel was marked, not by buoys, but by a series of massive tarry baulks driven into the sandbanks and mudflats on either side; the water was without currents, and so calm that there was no danger of these being uprooted. On top of each baulk sat a solemn bird—a pelican watching for fish. As we drew close to his perch, each sentry in turn would utter an indignant squawk, flop from his pedestal, recover himself just before he hit the water, and then fly heavily away, circling until we had removed ourselves to a safe distance from his chosen station.

Eventually we passed between the twin headlands and reached the sea itself, where sudden choppy waves made the boat lurch, and sent every hand reaching for a rail or some other support. It was the gulls who circled us now, greedily screeching, always on the look out for a tit-bit. The many ships that passed through this little stretch of water kept them well fed—they expected some offering from every boat that moved through it, even one as small as our own.

It was not long before we reached the islet where we were to picnic, and dropped anchor. The islet was one of a small group of coral knobs which had barely managed to raise themselves above the level of the sea. Any tide, had there been tides in the Caribbean, would have drowned them. Each passing hurricane would devastate them, and wash away every scrap of vegetation. Yet the birds, and seeds and weed brought by passing currents, saw to it that they survived. After every big storm, the coral knobs were re-seeded, and sprouted green again.

The islet we had chosen for our landfall was surrounded by a fine sandy beach, surprisingly clean and free of débris. Then came a little step up, a run of tumbled coral blocks, then, in the centre, a thicket of tangled spiny vegetation. You could walk around the island—its entire circumference was perhaps half a mile, but not across it. These were all plants which well knew how to defend themselves. The dry and leathery texture told one that, despite being surrounded by water, they still had to struggle to find enough water to live, in this place without a natural stream or spring.

Indeed, one soon discovered that, despite its idyllic air, the little island was not particularly friendly to visitors. The coral blocks, if recently broken, had edges which were razor-sharp. The rocks below water level were covered with sea-urchins. It was not long before one child had put a foot squarely down on one of these creatures. The brittle spines immediately broke off in the flesh.

The accident was so common that one of the adults at least had anticipated it. A candle was produced and lit, and the hot wax was allowed to drip down so as to cover the afflicted part. The victim, meanwhile, not unhappy to be the centre of everyone's attention, made a great parade of stoicism. It did not take long, in any case, for the thin layer of wax to cool. As soon as it was thoroughly crisp and stiff, a careful finger nail was used to pry it away from the skin in a single piece. There, projecting from the underside, was a cluster of little black points—the tips of the sea-urchin spines which would otherwise have festered and worked their way deeper. After being duly anointed with iodine, the unlucky child was soon hobbling about again.

The routine of such picnics never varied. First, lunch; then a circuit of the island; then a sleep and a swim, and then the return. By the time we made ready to go, it was an hour or less from sunset. It would be quite dark by the time we got back to the yacht-club jetty. The view as we returned was spectacular: the thickly forested mountains, streaked here and there with land-slips and gullies, heaved themselves up in front of us, turning from dark green to grape-purple, gradually getting darker as the light faded and as we got closer. As we came nearer and nearer to our destination, the lights of Kingston began to come on, and we could also see them twinkling mysteriously in the mountains, and the headlights of cars moving along distant roads.

Only one thing tended to spoil my pleasure in this spectacle —pressure on the bladder. I was an exceptionally modest child; I found it impossible to make water if I thought anyone was watching me. The thorny vegetation of the island had resisted any attempt to find a place of concealment. Now the way to the launch's tiny lavatory was blocked by jumbled picnic baskets and other impedimenta. In any case, I did not want to confess my plight. I knew that there were those present who might hold the story against me. With mounting desperation, I watched the shore coming very slowly closer to us. But somehow I managed to hold out.

CHAPTER FIVE

THE TIME WHEN I got on best with my contemporaries, however, was during occasional forays to the mountains. Jamaica has an equable climate, but in August the heat in Kingston can grow oppressive. The night-wind fails, the humidity rises, the air grows still and heavy. The thing to do was to rent, if you could get one, a house in the old mountain cantonment of Newcastle.

This was perched high above Kingston itself, in fact the mountains seemed to drop sheer down to the Liguanea plain, almost without the intervention of foothills. The roads to Newcastle were in those days steep and rough, surfaced with loose gravel, and liable to be blocked after a day's rain. The cantonment now consisted of a cluster of picturesquely inconvenient little houses, once designed, I suppose, to serve as officers' quarters. They had names appropriate to either their shape or their location. The Look Out was the highest—you couldn't get a car up there. The Race-Course stood on the old garrison race-course, now disused. The Ark was like an old-fashioned Noah's Ark, stranded on the ridge of Ararat. All the rooms in this house opened on to a single balcony, and none opened into another room. If you went to Newcastle, you accepted the fact that you would inhabit a kind of compromise between a house and a tent.

Nevertheless, the pleasures of the place were manifold. The air, three thousand feet up, was clear and sparkling—at least on those days which were free of rain. From the balconies of some of the houses one saw immense panoramas—Kingston, with its harbour and the surrounding suburbs. A yacht moving across the harbour sliced the water like a dress-maker's scissors cutting a piece of silk, and left a great spreading V-shaped tear behind it. A tractor moving in a sugar-cane field sent blinding signals, as the sunlight flashed from its windshield or metalwork. And then there were easy walks leading still higher into the mountains, along paths hemmed in by a marvellous confusion of vegetation, like a botanical garden run riot. Lime-trees, creepers, patches of ginger lilies, orchids, evil-looking fungi—one never knew what one would see next.

In good weather, the children in residence in the various houses ran freely from one to another. Somehow we were less fretful, and quarrelled less. This amity was sometimes strained when the rains came down. The clouds dashed themselves against the mountains and seemed to burst abruptly, letting fall water by bucketsful and barrelsful. It drummed on the roofs (many of which were made of tin sheeting, and greeted the assault with a joyful roar). It overflowed the gutters, washed out the roads, and short-circuited the electricity supply. Two or three days of real rain in Newcastle could mean almost a week's isolation.

Some means had to be found of keeping the children occupied under these conditions. Sometimes we played cards—whist or bezique or canasta. Very occasionally, if we could find the set, we played mah-jongg. Most commonly, however, we played Monopoly. In my mind's eye I can still see one of the big square rooms of the Ark, on an exceptionally wet day. The rain is beating noisily on the roof, and the windows are rattling. The lights have failed again, and there are stubby candles burning here and there in saucers. Because it seems chilly, our bare legs are thrust under communal blankets, as we sit on the floor round the board. It is I who am triumphing (in fact, I usually win on these occasions, but this time I am winning hand over fist). Every time anyone moves his counter, I seem to collect more money; I built more and more houses, exchange mediocre properties for better ones. The difficulty will be, I can see, to prevent one or other of the losers from interrupting the game before it is fully over: several faces are already begining to darken. But for the moment I want the rain to go on, so that the game can go on; and so, too, that there can be yet another game of Monopoly after that.

This particular day in Newcastle was, I suspect, during one of our later visits there, during a holiday from boarding school. Certainly, we were already deep in the war, which broke out when I was six. The war gradually made a great difference to the kind of social pattern which I have been describing. It probably changed the pattern for an only child, such as myself, most of all. Lack of petrol made it impossible to run the children back and forth to see one another, in the old style. Public transport scarcely existed in the Kingston suburbs, and no well-brought-up white child would have been allowed to travel on the buses alone —which is really to say no white child at all. When we were living in Kingston—which was most of the time—I was increasingly isolated from my contemporaries, just as I was increasingly isolated from my parents. We saw one another in the mornings, at nursery school, but this is an institution about which I recall curiously little—almost my only memory is one I have already described, my stately progress to it every day, with the garden-boy following behind.

I should have been almost entirely driven back on my own company but for the presence of the cook's niece, Lena. Lena did not live with Elma all the time, but for a long period she was with us more often than not. Though the cook described Lena as her niece, the relationship was left unspecific—it was impossible to tell, in fact, just how they were related to one another. Lena was about my own age, and she was attractive—lean (like her name), lithe, with a pale golden skin. She put up with my imperiousness with wonderful good humour. I never noticed then what I think I should have noticed now—a sophisticated detachment, a refusal to give up everything to the relationship which we soon formed, which was certainly a close one. For a while we were 'best friends', but in a curiously provisional way, quite unlike the other 'best friendships' which I recall from my childhood. She knew, and I in the end may have guessed, that our link was *ad hoc*, the product of special circumstances. It was Elma who grew worried when we seemed to be growing too close. She did not wish to upset the established order of things, and she would call Lena away and invent little duties for her when we appeared to be too much in one another's company. Later, when I went to school, Lena disappeared from the household. Her ambition, she often said, was to be a hospital nurse. I now and then wonder what happened to her, and whether she achieved it?

In a sense, I was not always sorry when Elma called Lena away.

The fantasy life I have spoken of—which had been with me from my earliest childhood—grew yet more powerful, if that were possible, rather than less. Now I less and less came to need the toys, the objects, the visible props which I have described. The imagination by itself was enough. And what the imagination fed upon was books.

I had learned to read both early and easily, and reading soon became an addiction. I was not particularly discriminating. I read *Winnie the Pooh* and *Alice in Wonderland* and *The Wind in the Willows* and Arthur Ransome's *We Didn't Mean to go to Sea.* Kipling's *Rewards and Fairies* and *Puck of Pook's Hill* were unearthed from among the limp leather-bound volumes decaying in the bedroom-passage. So too were *The Jungle Book* and *Just So Stories.* From this beginning I went on, as a matter of course, to read all the other volumes in the set. I didn't like all of them: some of them bored me because I didn't quite understand them, and some frightened or depressed me, and some (the more sadistic stories) excited me in a way that I found uncomfortable. Nevertheless I read them. Those I liked best I read several times over, with an intensity of experience which I have never been able to duplicate since. At the same time, I read every Superman comic I could lay my hands on—as soon as American servicemen started to arrive on the island, the comics came too.

Books gave me more pleasure than films. Indeed, it would be true to say that I disliked many films (I had to be taken out of *The Wizard of Oz*), because for me the vision was too real, and, because it had not been constructed bit by bit in my mind, seemed threatening and uncontrollable.

Some of my favourites were perhaps a little strange. Among her books my mother had quite a good stock of the best-sellers of the twenties and thirties. One of these was a large, once-popular and still admired volume called *Winged Pharaoh*, by Joan Grant. Miss Grant was a believer in reincarnation. She never made it entirely clear whether or not you were to read her narrative as presumed fact, or as fiction. At any rate, it was published as fiction. It was the exciting tale of the magical ordeals of an Egyptian princess, born into some early dynasty, and eventually called upon to rule over her country. Why this book struck home to me I have no idea, but strike home it did. I read it over and over.

A little after my discovery of Joan Grant, I was allowed to have a ticket to the Jamaica Institute Library, as my appetite for books had now completely outstripped the resources of the household. In spite of transportation difficulties, I would go down there to choose my reading matter for myself. One day, casting my eye over an unfamiliar block of shelves, I came across Howard Carter's two-volume account of the discovery and excavation of the tomb of Tutankhamun. I at once insisted on taking it out.

Once home, I opened it, and began to read. No one can claim that Carter is a sparkling prose-writer. His account, meticulous, minutely detailed, of what he found in the tomb, and where, might be thought to be tough going for a reader of such tender years. Not a bit of it. This, in a way, was the very book I had been looking for—full of material, seriously, lovingly described, but inert material, not yet arranged in patterns which were meant to have an emotional significance. From what I found in Carter's book, and taking a few hints from Miss Grant as well, I constructed a private world. I could lie in bed at night, stiff and straight like Tutankhamun in his coffin, and at the same time rise up, move *out* of myself, and walk through the bedroom wall at the front of the bed. On the other side of the wall was an Egyptian courtyard garden, with white walls divided by pilasters. In the centre of the courtyard was an oblong pool, with four great vases, one at each corner. In the pool were lotuses. On the pavement, in one corner, was a reed mat. It was possible to lie there and enjoy the dry air, and the quiet, and the clear sun. Usually, that was all that I did. Sometimes, however, I would go through another door, at the far end of the space, and walk into an Egyptian house, dim and cool, with splashes of light here and there from Tutankhamun's elaborate alabaster lamps, which were burning perfumed oils. And sometimes, but very rarely, I would walk through the house, and through the porch with its papyrus columns, and into the Egypt outside.

The characteristics of this fantasy were threefold—its privacy (I never spoke of it), its solitude (other people only appeared in it when I allowed myself to step through the portico, and then only in the distance), and its controllability. At any minute I could return myself back to the body which lay rigid upon the bed. I should emphasize too, that it was not a dream, but a true fantasy. I never visited that courtyard or that house when I was asleep.

Sleep, at this period, was not always welcome. Fantasies were even a means of putting it off. More even than most children I was reluctant to be sent to bed, and once in bed would cry out interminably and no doubt exasperatingly for another and yet another glass of water. I was afraid of the dark, and despite my leanings towards solitude, I was especially afraid of being left alone in the house. I often had nightmares, the more frightening because I remembered them only in fragments. Sometimes I would awaken in the small hours to find my sheets and pyjamas drenched through with sweat, as though I had been sleeping out in the dew. Meanwhile a tendril of creeper tapped at the frosted pane, and the headlights of cars passing by on the road outside the house lit up the glass with a glaring brightness, then swung away and faded again.

Strangely enough, I was not frightened on those occasions when there was really something to be afraid of. Jamaica is subject to earthquakes; once or twice during this period of my childhood I woke to feel the bed shaking violently under me, and to hear the bedroom door flapping and banging, while from outside there came a rumble both deeper and longer sustained than the rumble of thunder. None of this truly upset me: I pretended to be a little alarmed because other people were, it was the convention for the occasion. Hurricane weather pleased and excited me. I liked the disruption of routine, the faint fear that the violent wind would blow the windows in: one could see the rain spurting in a fine spray from the corners of the sashes, and the water piled up on the verandah, trickling under the french doors.

My other phobia, more constant and fiercer than my resistance to sleep (which was, despite all that I have said, only occasional) was my resistance to food. Mealtimes were the despair and the battleground of my childhood—not merely my despair and my battleground, but everybody's. One family story, doubtless apocryphal, has it that my life, when I was a newborn infant, was at one moment despaired of, because I refused to accept the bottle. Throughout my childhood I showed no enthusiasm at all for food, at least at the family table. Long battles took place at lunch and dinner, especially if my parents were present. I sat chewing the same nauseous mouthful of food over and over again, unable to bring myself to swallow it. Certain prejudices were early implanted. A struggle, when I was little more than a baby, over a plate of lukewarm white fish left me convinced that I was unable to eat fish of any kind without vomiting, a gastronomic quirk which was to play a catastrophic rôle during my schooldays. Every meal thus developed into a test of wills which was exhausting for both sides.

Obviously this stubborn distaste for food (or, rather, for the act of eating) must have been connected with some kind of psychological disturbance. I am unable to say whether it was simply a desire to draw attention to myself; or a refusal of love, as some people would have it. All I can now say is that what I remember, besides those interminable arguments, those exasperated cajolings as the spoon was once again lifted from the plate and then returned to it untouched, is that I felt a sense of oppression which I could never explain.

CHAPTER SIX

BY THIS TIME I was eight, and it was time to send me to boarding school. It was not an event I looked forward to with much confidence. I already knew that I did not get on with other children. If sides were being picked for some game involving two teams, it was always I who was left till last, the rotten banana at the bottom of the basket. I was convinced that school would be a place of imprisonment and terror. By and large, my sombre expectations were fulfilled.

The school itself was the best, or at least the most select, or one might almost say the only, boys' preparatory school on the island. It was situated in the elegant little resort town of Mandeville, a place for quiet retired couples, a kind of tropical Cheltenham. I believe the building which housed it had once been a hotel. This building had an impressive, but at the same time an absurd aspect. Perched high on a knoll, it looked like a steam-boat gothic version of the Tower of London. At each corner there was a turret. At first floor, and then again at second floor level, there were lacy balconies, intricate ribbons stretched between the corner-posts of the towers.

The school population was varied. It comprised the children of well-established planters, of government officials, of prosperous business men. Some showed what a generation prior to that of my parents, and somewhat more forthright, would have called 'a touch of the tar brush'. As an institution the place must at that period have stood—indeed, it could hardly help but stand—for the maintenance of the kind of division I have already described, the division between the world that 'people like us' belonged to, and the very different world of the people outside. Yet this barrier was already being eroded; even the most conservative recognized that, in its present form at least, it could not be maintained for much longer. At the same time, the school reflected the merciful West Indian double-think about colour, which was in all respects typical of the people who chose to send their children there. In Jamaica, to a limited but nevertheless significant extent, you were white if you thought you were. In this situation, the small but rich Asian community often assumed a mediating rôle. Among my school-mates, for example, were to be found two tough Chinese brothers whose surname was Henderson.

Strangely enough, colour was the one subject about which no boy was teased or bullied by another. We all agreed, even the roughest, even the crassest, that the topic must be left alone. Apart from that, all cruelties were permitted. My little companions soon discovered that I was a natural butt.

It is easy enough to remember that one was miserable, but mercifully harder to recall the precise details of how one was made miserable. Certainly I was pinched, teased and bullied all day long. I was afraid to go to the lavatories, for fear of being trapped there by some tormentor, and was afflicted as a result with self-induced constipation. But food was the thing that gave the easiest and most effective opportunities to my persecutors, who were most of them the rough boys from the 'up-country' plantations, used to being little kings on their parents' estates. My aversion to fish was soon discovered. The day we had sardines was a day of terror—ambushes were laid in order to try to force one down my throat. On one occasion, a teacher decided to join in. It had been arranged that I was to have a special diet when fish was served—it was thus, indeed, that my weakness had been discovered. This master, impatient and sceptical rather than actually cruel, decided that the concession was nevertheless to be withdrawn. He stood over me, while the hated nourishment went down between thick slices of bread, which served to muffle the nauseating flavour. When the last scrap had vanished, he embarked on a tirade on not giving in to one's imagination. I interrupted this, just when it was reaching its climax, by being resoundingly sick. For once I scored a triumph. When I looked up from my vomit, the poor man had vanished. By him, at least, the subject was never mentioned again.

I must not, by telling this story, give the impression that the staff were unkind to me. They were not, whatever their occasional oddities, the Dickensian ushers who tormented the little boys of the nineteenth century. But they were curiously blind to what was going on—and I could not tell them directly for fear of being labelled a 'sneak', thus making matters still worse for myself.

I tried various ways of dealing with the situation—not selected as coldly as the phrase might suggest, of course. They were the ploys of instinct, but ploys nevertheless. The first, easiest and most obvious, was to fall sick. I developed a knack of running a slight temperature almost at will. The school-matron, a gruff woman who resembled an elderly wire-haired terrier, was puzzled by the frequency with which I managed to produce these temperatures, and would stare at the thermometer unbelievingly. Sometimes she would accuse me of dipping it into hot water, or shaking it while her back was turned. But a second reading, taken while she sat and glared at me, would invariably confirm the first. Grumbling, she would tell me to get my things and put myself to bed in the sickroom. Here at least I was safe for a day or two.

A second ploy was that adopted by Schéhérazade. I could not hope to improve my fortunes by triumphing at games—I had soon discovered that I had no eye for a ball, in addition to being generally clumsy and slow in my movements. But much reading had, I also found, turned me into an adept story-teller. The first opportunity given to me for a really extended exercise of this skill came when the school was swept by a double epidemic of 'flu and chickenpox. Those affected were banished to the school sanatorium—a separate building at the back of the main block. I dreaded being sent there, as I knew that the inmates were very little supervised, and would therefore be even freer to torment me than they were under ordinary school conditions. But the day came when my rash of spots could no longer be concealed, and off I went, like a prisoner to the torture-chamber. The nights, after lights out, were the worst times. In order to keep my persecutors at bay, I began to tell an elaborate adventure serial in many parts, based on the gorier war-comics which I had read. Any assault meant the instant interruption of the story, and a tearful refusal to resume it. For some reason my narrative proved so compelling that I was, by and large, left alone.

It might be easy to look back a little nostalgically to these evenings of narrative, with the fireflies darting about on the rough hillside outside the sanatorium windows (sometimes the temptation would prove to be too much, and we would rush outside, in pyjamas and bare feet, to try to catch them). And I suppose that it would also be easy to dismiss this account of persecution as exaggeration, as being something which is likely to happen to all spoilt only children when they first go to boarding school. I wonder, still, if this verdict is not a little too comfortable, too easy?

Looking back, I believe I learned a number of things from this unhappy period—not least among them secretiveness and self-consciousness. After my first year at school, just as I was due to return for another miserable term, I burst into tears on the last night of the holidays, and begged to be taken away. This request was refused, as indeed I think I had expected it to be. After all, where else was there to send me? Where else, at any rate, that was suitable? Yet, at the same time, as I realized after I had failed to gain my point, the request had also been made as a kind of test, to see if anyone could diagnose what was wrong with me. The experiment failed, and I took the burden of its failure on myself, resolving thereafter to be my own master, my own responsibility.

During my second year at school, my father became seriously ill. Playing polo, he fell heavily, and the fall seemed to upset his whole system. At last, after much puzzlement, cancer of the lung was diagnosed, and my mother had to accompany him to America, so that a major operation could be performed. During my father's long illness, my parents, through force of circumstances, drifted further and further away from me. Little news filtered through from them, and such of it as reached me was unspecific. I spent the Christmas holidays with friends, part of it at King's House, as the guest of the governor, one of whose sons was a contemporary of mine, and was at school with me. The government house routine seemed an extension, on a much larger and grander scale, of what was already familiar from our own household. At lunchtimes we all—governor, governor's

lady, ADCs, members of the staff, assorted guests and children—
sat at an immense mahogany dining table in an equally huge
banqueting room, trying to find some topic of conversation
which was suitable to everybody. The governor himself was a
man of exquisite but formidable politeness, and talk was expected
to be general. From a child's point of view the difficulties of
keeping one's end up were increased by the behaviour of the
government house spaniel, which had a vast, sack-like mouth and
a passion for the whiting on the tennis shoes which we wore. One
would be in the midst of answering some courteous, complicated
and lofty question from His Excellency, when suddenly one's foot
would be suffused with a warm wetness which meant that the
spaniel had crept under the table, and had taken one's entire shoe
into his mouth.

After this interlude, I returned to school, to confront the bullies
once again. It was now getting close to my tenth birthday—my
birthday fell at the end of February—and the news came that my
father was back, and that both my parents would be coming to
Mandeville to take me out. I was to ask a dozen or so of my little
friends out to tea, to a local teashop which served a famous straw-
berry shortcake. The guest list was carefully prepared, after a
distinctly political fashion, since it included a good number of my
enemies—those who seemed most easily susceptible to the attrac-
tions of a good blow-out, and most likely to be grateful afterwards. The party went off in high spirits, but only my mother
appeared at it. My father was 'too tired' to come.

It was now so long since I had seen him that I took this news
with what must have seemed like indifference. In fact, I felt a pin-
prick of foreboding. A little more than a week later, this foreboding was to be confirmed. I suddenly received a summons to
go and see the headmaster. Drearily, I trudged up the long flight
of stairs to his study. The headmaster was an impressive figure, a
clergyman, very tall, completely bald, with a pale sapphire in a
gold band on his little finger. His study was dark, and reeked of
the tobacco which he kept in a mottled brown stoneware jar on a
shelf above his desk. The gleaming highlights on the shoulders of
the jar and on the crown of his bald dome moved simultaneously
when you looked at them. He gazed at me, with pale eyes the

colour of the stone on his finger, and told me abruptly that my father was dead. Once again, as so often in the immediate past, I burst into floods of tears.

Yet even as I cried, I knew that I was something of a fraud. By this time I scarcely knew my father. As I have said, even before I went to boarding school I saw little of him. Now I had not seen him for more than a year, and I suddenly realized that I found it difficult to remember even what he looked like. At the same time, almost before the news had had time to sink in, I found myself calculating what its impact on my own situation would be. Nobody, said a voice at the back of my mind, would feel inclined to bully a little boy whose father had just died—and if they did happen to make such a mistake, then it would be a simple matter to turn the whole pack against them. Having reached this conclusion, I started to cry harder than ever, forcing the tears out in great racking gasps. Somewhat startled by the violence of my reaction, the headmaster sent me off to matron to recover myself. She, poor soul, was sympathetic. She did not know that what made the tears flow was chiefly a sense of relief.

The great test of my notion that this family loss would bring me immediate benefit was school assembly the next morning. We all crowded into the large class room where brief prayers were said, homilies were given, and routine announcements were made. I knew that the headmaster would be bound to say something about my father's death. But I knew, too, that the news would already have travelled round the school. Deliberately I hung back as the rest of the boys crowded in. As I entered among the latecomers every eye turned towards me. In almost all, I saw a gleam of respect.

Later—much later—I was to write a poem about my father's death and my own reaction to it. It appeared in my first book of verse, *A Tropical Childhood* which was published in 1961, and did not seem to attract any special attention. Gradually, however, it began to gain in popularity, and became better and better known through anthologies, most of them designed for schools. The more often it appears in these collections, the more requests for permission to reprint I seem to receive. I often wonder what explanations teachers offer their pupils about it.

After my father's death, and the respite I gained from it, my situation gradually improved. I was now notably self-contained, and therefore much less satisfactory as a subject for teasing. And I was becoming a dangerous opponent—not so much physically, as there were still many boys who were bigger and stronger than I—but in any kind of slanging match. I discovered a gift for inventing nick-names, and for propagating them once invented. Any puppy-dog who barked at me was likely to find a tin can tied to his tail. And of course, each new term meant a fresh intake of potential victims. You could spot them a long way off—the soft, the vulnerable, the uncertain. There was Bobby, for example, who still wet his bed; and Sammy, the most hapless of the lot. It was difficult to say why Sammy attracted bullying, except that he was clumsy and had a tendency to run into things rather than round them. In fact, he proved too vulnerable to last. He survived his schooling with us, but I afterwards heard (I still don't know whether or not it is true) that at his next educational establishment Sammy's school-fellows one day chased him up a tree. He lost his grip, fell out of it, and was killed.

CHAPTER SEVEN

IT WOULD GIVE a false impressions to describe my first boarding school entirely in terms of bullying and being bullied. As an establishment, it had a number of eccentric aspects which are endearing to look back on, though some were less acceptable at the time. One can even laugh a little about the food, though this, even apart from the hated sardines, was certainly the most horrible I have ever tasted. The menu moved in stately procession, changing from one day to the next, but always repeating itself exactly after the passage of a complete week. We always knew what we were due to get. On Monday, the Yellow Peril; on Tuesday, Aeroplane Accident; on Wednesday, Dead Dog and Boiled Snake; on Thursday, Fishes' Eyes. Since the names are not entirely self-explanatory, I ought to explain that the Yellow Peril, for instance, was scrambled dried egg, while Dead Dog and Boiled Snake was a peculiarly fatty form of mince accompanied by over-cooked spaghetti.

I was never, then or later, able to make out why the food was so nasty—although it was wartime, we had no rationing in Jamaica, such as was to be found in England. In 1946, at my English boarding school, the food was even a slight improvement over the kind of institutional cooking I was already used to.

A further disadvantage, where this horrid nourishment was concerned, was the fact that we were forced to eat up every scrap. The school dining-hall was a long, narrow hall which ran across the back of the main building on the ground floor. It was just wide enough to take two rows of long tables. Half the company, therefore, sat with their backs pressed against the walls, while half sat with their backs turned to the long alleyway which ran down the middle. There was always fierce competition for seats against the wall, because here, in case of need, you could dispose of what you didn't like by dropping it under the table, or even, if you knew where to put your fingers, by shoving it through one of the numerous mouse-holes to be found in the skirting boards. The mice in that building grew fat. If you came into the deserted dining-hall after meals, you could sometimes see them skittering down the polished tables, or bouncing from the benches to the floor.

Particularly finicky eaters, such as myself, had the doubtful honour of being placed next to the headmaster, or to some other teacher, so that he or she could supervise what was consumed. At one period I found myself condemned for long periods to the post of chief danger, which was the seat on the end of the bench nearest to the headmaster and on his left—that is, with my back to the aisle. Seated here, it required the very greatest sleight of hand to get rid of some unwanted morsel. But here, too, my talents as a Schéhérazade—and also my efforts to maintain a proper level of general conversation at the King's House luncheon table—stood me in good stead. In fact, the headmaster and I got on reasonably well: the discovery had just been made that I was clever. We talked, or, rather, the game was to make him talk, while one listened, apparently rapt, to what he had to say. The sign that he was well away was the metronomic beat of the fork in his left hand, the ring upon his little finger twinkling as the hand itself moved. Once this rhythm was established, it was possible to begin slipping little bits of meat from one's plate to the floor, where they could then be forced through a wide crack in the boards with a rubbing motion of the heel of one's shoe. I was never caught doing this.

One great fount of eccentricity in the school was the teaching staff. The headmaster had few foibles, and no really startling ones. But it was wartime, and he had great difficulty in finding, and keeping, suitable teachers. Those who educated us were a motley crew—the too young, the too old, and the women. Tempted out of his retirement to try to instil a little knowledge into us was Mr Mackeson, silvery-haired, distinguished, with a well-cut but distinctly threadbare white tropical suit, a monocle and a panama hat. His blue eyes were watery; his cheeks above his goatee were innocently rosy. No doubt unjustly, we boys were convinced that he drank. He aroused our jeering laughter with one particular habit. Hands in pockets was the thing he detested. It was un-gentlemanly, so he assured us in frequent harangues. 'And most of all, never rattle money in your pockets, boys,' he would say, head thrown back, eye-glass gleaming, hands thrust deep in his own pockets, where keys and coins frantically jingled.

The gentlest but least effective of the ladies was Mrs Weinberger —a German-Jewish refugee. She taught, or attempted to teach, languages, but I think we rapidly defeated her. Her previous job, I seem to remember, had been driving a taxi somewhere in West Africa. Nevertheless, she came from a cultivated, and even a wealthy, background. Several times, just before the war, she had risked her life to smuggle jewels out of Germany for friends. 'How did you do it?' I asked her. 'Oh, it was quite simple,' she said. 'They were diamond brooches so big that all I had to do was to pin them to a cheap coat. Everyone thought they must be paste.' She herself still had a few trinkets left, coral pendants and such, which she would turn out of a cardboard box to show me.

Made of sterner stuff, and a better teacher, was a Canadian lady with a Scottish name. She had acquired this name by marriage, and her son Louis attended the school. Louis was tall, snub-nosed, freckled, taciturn. He wore shoes which fascinated the rest of us, with broad toes, and immensely thick crêpe-rubber soles. We had never seen anything like them before. His mother was fond of holding forth in class about the distinction of her son's ancestry. 'My son *Lou*-ie,' she would say, in her emphatic Canadian accent, meanwhile extending a rigid hand and forearm towards him, 'My son *Lou*-ie is the *chief* of a Scottish *tribe!*' Louis blushed, bowed his head and remained silent. There did not seem to be much else he could do.

The Canadian lady carried her loyalty to all things Scottish to the point of wearing a kilt, presumably in her husband's tartan, on every possible occasion. These kilts were distinctly short for the fashions of the 1940s, even if not nearly as brief as the later miniskirts were to be. In the senior class, to which I by this time belonged, the teacher sat perched on a high stool. Characteristically, Mrs MacKenzie would stamp into the room, plant herself on this, spread her legs wide, and sail into the lesson. I don't think she ever guessed why there was such a rush to sit in the front rows when she was in charge of us. We were just beginning to be interested in sex, and the tightly stretched area of pink lisle knicker which she thus unwittingly exposed intrigued us enormously.

Any teacher who fell foul of the wolf-pack was liable to suffer for it. One teacher, a youngish and inexperienced man, offended us particularly. He had a habit, perhaps out of sheer nervousness, of picking on one member of the class, and of exposing him to a barrage of sarcasm. This habit first irritated and then outraged us. It was decided that we must act collectively. A number of us wrote an identical round-robin letter to our parents to complain. The result, predictably, was a spectacular explosion. Yet there was little the headmaster could do about it: he might feel that the master himself had been incautious, he might feel that those who had complained were a lot of little villains. But no real action could be taken. Unwisely, the master complained and sulked, rather than trying to resolve the situation.

I had been one of the ring-leaders in organizing the round-robin letter. I now persuaded my school-mates to embark on guerrilla action. Perched on its knoll, the building offered a clear view of playgrounds and playing-fields. Mr Brown, his troubles weighing on his mind, was apt to patrol the balconies nervously, with an eye open to see what we were up to. Very well, we would let him see something worth looking at. Every time Mr Brown appeared, we rushed to form a knot or huddle, whispering excitedly. Every time he approached, we separated with a guilty air. If he seized one of us, and asked to know what we had been saying, the answer was always a stolid 'Nothing, sir'. And indeed we *had* been saying nothing—our whisperings were all gibberish. A few days of this treatment were enough. We extracted a kind of apology, and normal relations were resumed.

I mentioned, a little earlier, that it had now been discovered that I was 'clever'. I don't think that I showed much aptitude for school work when I first went to boarding-school, perhaps because I was then too much badgered and bullied to pay much

attention to it; perhaps, simply, because I had not yet acquired
the habit of work. But it now began to be noticed that I was good
at my books. My widowed mother was planning to leave the
island once the war was over: I would then be of an age to be sent
to an English boarding school. It began to be thought, and even
said, that I was capable of winning a scholarship.

The difficulty was that I was much better at some subjects than
at others. My mathematics, in particular, were unreliable. Fortunately, a suitable tutor was living in a cottage just at the school
gates—Miss Moren, retired from teaching at the island's leading
girls' school. Miss Moren had a weak heart, hers were the clayey
complexion and pale lips of some sufferers from heart disease.
But there was nothing weak about her otherwise. She was a
magnificent teacher, the first really gifted one into whose hands
I had fallen. We would sit down together in her bare little room,
and she would firmly pull down the blind, in case even the sunshine sparkling in the garden should distract me. In the course of
a couple of terms she managed to put more mathematical
knowledge into me than anyone has managed to do since—indeed, when I eventually won my scholarship, my excellent maths
were said to have played a large part in the decision to award it
to me. Unfortunately, what she put in quickly leaked away again
when I was forced to cover the same ground all over again in
England. But it was the scholarship itself that was important,
indeed vital. There is, too, another debt that I owe to Miss Moren
—she taught me the pleasure of learning something, which is also
the pleasure of being taught. It has been one of the most lasting
and reliable of my life.

As my situation at school improved, so I was able to look outside it again, to become what people would call 'a normal little
boy', though of a rather timorous variety. After my father's death
my mother took a full-time job, and she also decided to move
house. The new house, oddly enough in the circumstances, was
rather larger and grander than the one we had previously occupied, though built to very much the same pattern. It had two
bathrooms, for example, rather than one. In the holidays, I
rattled around in it, like a pebble in a can.

This situation did not last long. The war was now at its height.

Even here in the Caribbean, perhaps the peacefullest remaining area of the world, it rumbled louder and louder off stage. My mother's new job was connected with information and propaganda. Once or twice I went to see her at her office in downtown Kingston, and was fascinated by the great piles of black plastic oblongs which lay scattered around in it. These were blocks for distribution to the newspapers. If you tilted the plastic so that the light glided across its surface, you could see, in black on black, pictures of tanks in the desert or of aircraft crashing in flames. One of my mother's occasional jobs was to read the news—her clear, very English voice negotiated the strange syllables, names of places in Russia, or Tunisia, or of specks of coral in the Pacific, with surprising aplomb.

As the war grew and spread, more and more officers came to Jamaica. The cocktail parties were noisier and gayer than ever, though the complaint was that it was hard to get whisky—you had to drink rum. These newly arrived officers also found it hard to find places for their families to live.

One of them was an English captain, rather dashing, with a pretty, willowy American wife. They had three boys: one two years younger than I was, one two years younger still, and one who was almost a baby. They moved in with us for a while and, from being rather empty, the new house was suddenly full.

The three brothers became the siblings I had never had—for, surprisingly enough, I felt no resentment at being dethroned from my position as an only child. The chief reason for this lack of friction was the eldest of the brothers, who was called Victor. Victor immediately became my best friend. Indeed, it would not be too much to say that I fell in love with him.

He was very pale, and transparently fair, with hair so flaxen that it was almost white. Bugs loved Victor: if there was one anywhere nearby it came rushing to bite him. Germs loved Victor, too—he had a low resistance to them. He was the first to catch 'flu in any minor epidemic; every smallest cut or scratch had a tendency to turn septic. Many plants were also hostile to him: if he went for a country walk he usually came out in a rash. Yet despite all this he was sturdily-built, vigorous, noisy, straightforward: he attracted love as powerfully as he attracted eager germs and insects.

We were never out of one another's company; we galloped round the house together, we teased and petted his brothers, we romped with the dogs, we rolled on the floor and were breathless with laughter. Victor was sent to my school, and it was the same situation there. Whenever I was with Victor I was perfectly happy. Loneliness vanished, and so did calculation.

In addition to sharing the house, we all of us spent our holidays together. Once, it was in Newcastle. I initiated Victor into my elaborate fantasies. My games, by this time, were largely connected with the war. I now had a huge collection of lead soldiers, and of model tanks and guns and aeroplanes—many more toys than the brothers had been able to bring with them from America. Victor and I spent all the daylight hours in the small garden attached to our holiday cottage. Since the house itself was built into the side of a hill, the garden comprised a series of terraces, walks, built-up flower beds and little paths, all of them much neglected and overgrown with weeds. It was an excellent terrain for the creation of a miniature landscape. We tunnelled into the banks, made huts of twigs and encampments of scraps of cloth. Roads were created, and laboriously paved with pebbles, and then were washed out again, if the rules of the game required it, with a deluge from a watering-can. Even inside the house there were camouflaged aerodromes under our beds, and the model planes ran on wires from corner to corner of the room. Murray, the next in age of Victor's two brothers, was a frequent victim of airborne sneak attacks—one of us would lure him under the wire; the other would release the mechanism to bring a heavy model swooping down to crack him on the head.

Another holiday, the very last, was spent at an almost derelict coffee-plantation. This, too, was in the mountains, but it did not have the sweeping views one got from the cantonment houses at Newcastle. The estate lay in a kind of pocket. From the front gate, one looked up and saw five little viaducts to mark the five turns the road made as it zigzagged its way up the mountain.

For some reason, I do not remember this holiday well, nor

even how long the brothers were with us. What I do recall is that the atmosphere was clouded and melancholy, though the war was nearly over and the wireless bleated about the triumphs the Allies were winning in Europe and in the Pacific. I already knew that we were going to leave the island soon; every day was a farewell. Yet many of the things we did on this occasion were things we had never done before. We went down to the place where the wooden sieves were that had been used for grading the coffee —dried berries were still stuck in the crevices, and we pried these out, and roasted them, and ground them in an old mill, and drank the result, feeling as proud as if we had grown the beans ourselves. And there was a fast-running stream where we hunted for the fresh-water crayfish Jamaicans call *jonghas*. The technique is to wade upstream, turning the larger stones over with feet and hands, and catching the shell-fish as they scuttle out.

Occasionally this stream widened into a pool deep enough to swim in, and icy cold, far colder than the sea we were used to. While we swam, the dachshund barked in a panic on the bank, sure that we were drowning.

The last day of all was spoilt by a stupid accident. I had made a model boat from the hard husk of a large nut, with a leaf for sail. The mast was a big darning-needle borrowed from my mother. Putting the model down on my bedroom chest of drawers as the packing was being done, I forgot that it was there, and for some reason banged my forearm down on the flat surface. The needle passed, eye foremost, between the two bones of the arm, and buried itself full length. It did not hurt as I drew it out again, and there was only a drop of blood, but the muscle throbbed ferociously for a week afterwards.

Despite the melancholy of this holiday, I had no idea that I would never see Victor again. But once we all left the island —his family to return to America, we ourselves headed for England—we soon dropped out of touch. We had not yet reached the age when one makes an effort to maintain an old friendship, even if it cannot be kept at its former level. Our parents, never, perhaps, really such friends as we had been, but, rather, the allies of circumstance, did not maintain contact. Some years after we had settled in England, the rumour reached us that Victor was

dead—a victim of one of the last big polio epidemics in the United
States. Despite his vitality, the news didn't seem altogether sur-
prising. The bugs and the germs asserted their rights and got poor
Victor in the end.

CHAPTER EIGHT

THE MOVE TO England broke my childhood in two. It co-incided with the onset of puberty; and, in any case, the contrast between the two modes of existence was in many ways drastic. Growing up in the tropics became, almost immediately, a subject for nostalgic reverie, and this nostalgic mood was something I maintained throughout my adolescence, and until well into my twenties. It colours many of the poems in my first book of verse, including the title-poem, 'A Tropical Childhood':

> That was the time when a dead grasshopper
> Devoured by ants before my captive eye
> Made the sun dark, yet distant battles were
> Names in a dream, outside geography.

One might say with some truth that I started inventing the myth, as soon as I had lost the place.

The ship we travelled on was our first introduction to post-war austerity. It was a banana-boat, originally designed to carry twelve passengers in addition to its cargo of fruit. Now there were over forty. If you took your bottom off a chair in the saloon, even for an instant, you were lucky to find a place to sit down again.

I had dim recollections of previous Atlantic crossings, and of England itself. My parents had had a home leave in 1938, when I was five. The ship, then, had seemed to me rather fun. I recalled a big staircase, which heaved and twisted, while one's own body stayed in the same place. I had no memory at all of ever being seasick. England, on the other hand, I remembered much less favourably. There were flannel shorts that chafed the inside of my thighs, and shoes that pinched my feet (at home, at least inside the house, I never wore shoes). My English nanny took me to see the Changing of the Guard, and we visited the statue of Peter Pan in Kensington Gardens. I played with a toy car on a violently patterned carpet, close to a gas-fire which toasted your front while it left your backside freezing. If you didn't have sixpence to put in it, it went out altogether. The streets of London were long and straight, and rarely was there anything interesting at the end of them. My parents had enjoyed their leave, but I endured it.

The crossing, this time, gave me a nasty surprise. Two or three days out the weather grew rough, and I began to feel queasy. At first I would not admit this feeling, even to myself. Seasickness was for other people. Inexorably the sensation gained on me. An incident one lunch-time was my definitive undoing. My mother had agreed to act as escort for another small boy, a contemporary of mine who was also going to England for his schooling, but without his parents. Fortunately Marcus and I got on well enough —we had discovered, for one thing, that we made a formidable whist partnership. Sitting next to me at table, he reached for a roll and broke it open. Entombed within it, like a pharaoh in his sarcophagus, was a very large and very dead cockroach. I got up, and rushed on deck, making for the rail.

Seasickness is one of the very few things in life which produces sensations which are, in the strict sense of the word, indescribable. I am told that in this respect it resembles childbirth, though of course in a minor key. So I will not dwell on my sufferings on this occasion, except to say that they had one feature which still strikes me as odd. However nauseated I felt, I longed for cheese. The longing existed, so to speak, in complete detachment from the nausea. Even now I cannot eat a certain sort of processed cheddar without recalling that passage across the Atlantic.

A few days before we reached port—the whole voyage took nearly a fortnight—the weather moderated, and we sailed up the Channel in brilliant sunshine. The sea, here, was still littered with wrecks, and their masts poked out of the water as melancholy reminders of the war which was only just over, and of the destruction we were to see when we reached dry land.

Our first night in England was spent at the De Vere Hotel in Kensington. It seemed a return to the England I had known in

1938. Large plate glass windows, lavishly lace-curtained, over-looked Kensington Gardens. Peter Pan was only just out of sight. On the bedroom chest-of-drawers were vases of tulips and daffodils, still tightly in bud, which had been given to us by my aunt, who had arranged our stay here. In the dankly chilly lounges, at tea-time, elderly waiters manœuvred trolleys loaded with cream cakes.

Soon enough, however, we had to leave this refuge, and we discovered that settling in England was not going to be easy. We had missed the war; and the pattern of life, in war's immediate aftermath, was one shaped by events we had not experienced. The catchword of the time was Austerity, a noun associated with the stern personality of Sir Stafford Cripps, whose scolding pro-nouncements took up a great deal of space in the few pages the newspapers were allowed to print. Austerity tended to be even more unremittingly austere for us newcomers than for those who had endured the combat.

In the first place, quite simply, we were not used to it. Every time we encountered them, stringencies and shortages affected us anew—with surprise, as well as with inconvenience and de-privation. In the second place, we had not yet achieved a niche in the system created by Austerity itself. The rations were the same for everybody, and everybody got the same number of clothing coupons. But, even if you were unwilling to take the plunge into a flourishing black market, or had no hope of affording its luxuries, you needed contacts, alliances, ways of bending the rules. It helped, for example, if your butcher was still the butcher you had gone to in the Blitz. It helped if you had remained in touch with the farmer to whom your children had gone as evacuees. We had none of these advantages. In addition to this, we were naïve, and perhaps a little arrogant in the colonial way. The tones of our voices, the very gestures we made, were wrong, and tended to give offence. The worn, weary, impatient people we met had no time for niceties; officials, in particular, were happy to bully ignorant newcomers such as ourselves. In Jamaica, we now realized, the clock had stopped at the end of the thirties; we found ourselves transported, not merely to a different country, but to a new and sterner decade.

However, this fact was concealed from us, at least to begin with. After my first term at school, we went to spend the start of the summer holidays with friends who had a house in North Cornwall. The wife was Jamaican born, married to an English Army officer, and we therefore shared much the same background. Cornwall was untouched by the war, and any exotic features to be discovered there were both obvious and pleasingly traditional. The things which made the greatest impression on me were the strange conical hills of St Austell. The artificial landscape created by the china clay industry seemed symbolic of our abrupt transfer to a new world. Later, it seemed that other symbols would have been more to the point.

Throughout our time in Cornwall, the weather was stormy. The gymkhana we went to was almost drowned out. We were often mewed up in the house. When we went for a drive, our host nursing the car along on rationed petrol, it was to see the sea beating on the black granite of the Cornish rocks and the lead coloured clouds racing through the skies above an equally leaden ocean. The local paper often carried news of wrecks. These accounts excited both the son of the household, who was about my age, and myself. We wanted to go and comb the beaches nearby, in the hope of finding romantic or useful bits of flotsam. These wishes were wisely frustrated by the grown-ups.

Later in that rainy summer, we lived for a while at a guest-house at Ashtead in Surrey. A school-friend had now joined us: my mother had agreed to act as his guardian during part of his stay in England: he was to be educated at the same school as the one I had already entered. Neither Paul nor I liked it much at Ashtead. The main cause of our complaint was that we were forced to share a bed—a large, lumpy double bed with a central ridge in the mattress, which then dipped away towards the edge on either side. This meant that the occupants, as they slept, tended to roll away from one another, each clutching the blankets. Paul was stronger than I was, and I often woke shivering in the small hours to find all the bedclothes gone, cocooned around the body of my sleeping companion, and to hear the perpetual dreary rain tapping on the window as the sky lightened and a few discouraged birds began to chirp.

The bedroom was heavily Victorian, as was the rest of the house. The drawing-room was a large, dim aquarium, where the pallid guests swam, never quite meeting, never quite conversing. The furniture ranged from massive objects in rosewood to spindly tables in lacquer and bamboo. I was always being chased out of it, as it was supposed I would get up to some mischief. In fact, I liked it because it was quiet; and because it was possible to be alone there. The regiments of little glass cabinets, not to mention the dank cold, kept intruders at bay. When I succeeded in isolating myself for a while, I read with my usual concentration. At this period I was reading the same book over and over again—*The Unquiet Grave*, Cyril Connolly's pseudonymous lament for a civilization which had vanished before I could get to know it. His slim anthology of nostalgic diary-jottings and despairing quotations from the classics was at that time the book of the moment with adults, though none of them at Ashtead could understand the fascination it held for me. For that matter, I didn't understand my own obsession with it, though I guess now that somewhere in that brief text lay the words and phrases which sparked off my desire to become a writer.

Evenings at Ashtead were usually spent in the billiard room, a vast chamber lined with mustard-coloured lincrusta wallpaper. Vigorous games of snooker would be played on the lumpy old billiard-table while either Paul or I marked the score. During these evenings I began to be wracked with the terrible boredom of adolescence. It differed from that of childhood because not only was I bored here, but I knew I would be bored elsewhere. I envisaged the worst tracts of the surrounding metroland, and told myself, with Byronic self-absorption, that these would be the setting for the rest of my life.

In fact, there was a good deal of beautiful parkland near the house, and we often went for walks in it. It was here that I became aware of something disconcerting. I no longer knew the names of things. Trees, wild flowers, the very features of everything: I thought I perceived them as keenly as ever, but was unable to store them safely in my mind for want of suitable labels. This was a deficiency which I have never quite been able to remedy. The Jamaican landscape can still be re-created in the mind by reciting a sort of litany—breadfruit, ackee, cashew, tamarind, soursop, mango: each of these is a tree with its own habit of growth, and not merely produce laid out on a market stall. But I could not then, and cannot now, do the same for a given stretch of English countryside: the magical act of re-creation is a failure either because I do not have the words, or, possessing them, cannot relate them to what I have seen.

CHAPTER NINE

IN TRYING TO describe the initial impact the move to England made on me, I have skipped over my arrival at my new school. The great terror of our uprooting, so far as I was concerned, had been the prospect of a change of schools. Having established myself safely and comfortably at prep school, I dreaded the initiation ceremonies I might have to endure, starting at the bottom of the ladder in a new and larger institution. My ideas of English public school life had largely been formed by reading *Stalky & Co.* Kipling's book of school stories, which I had encountered while ploughing through the complete works, exercised a horrid fascination over me; and of all the little limp leather volumes, this was the one which I re-read the most often.

The school chosen for me was King's School, Canterbury, chiefly because it offered scholarships which were reserved for the sons of colonial civil servants. It would be a struggle to educate me on a widow's civil service pension, and on what my mother could earn. As far as possible, I must pay my own way. I arrived for the summer term, on the understanding that I would sit the scholarship examination while already on the roster as a pupil.

The school buildings clustered, as they had for many centuries, around two great courtyards at the side of Canterbury Cathedral. The courtyards are called, respectively, the Mint Yard and the Green Court. They occupy the sites of former monastic edifices, and many of the buildings have remnants of medieval work built into their structure. Some are almost wholly medieval. When I arrived, some of the school buildings were in the process of being repaired or rebuilt—they had been damaged in the Baedeker raids on Canterbury. The school itself had only just returned from a war-time exile in a Cornish hotel.

Public school literature is so rich for the period preceding the

Second World War that one forgets, I think, how little has been written about them since. The social revolution which was supposed to dispose of them altogether has largely passed them by, though every now and again there is another threat to abolish them. At the same time, those who have passed through it no longer bring the same emotion to the discussion, or, more usually, the denunciation of the public school system. This makes it difficult to write about my time at King's. The reader will have to listen for nuances I may not be aware of myself.

Another thing which makes it difficult to write about my time at King's is the fact that, apart from Eton and perhaps Harrow, this is already the most literary of public schools, in the sense that a number of well-known writers have attended it, and most of them have left accounts, more or less disguised, of the time they spent there. Among these alumni were Hugh Walpole and Somerset Maugham, both of whom appear to have been miserable. Another, earlier, and to me more interesting pupil, was Walter Pater, whose novella, *Emerald Uthwart*, is, in some pages, the memorial to the time he spent at Canterbury.

I have just been re-reading it, preparatory to writing this chapter. Many passages show how little the place had changed between his time and mine. He describes, for example, how:

the scholars are taken to church in their surplices, across the court, under the lime-trees; emerge at last up the dark winding passages into the melodious, mellow-lighted space, always three days behind the temperature outside, so thick are the walls;—how warm and nice! how cool and nice! The choir, to which they glide in order to their places below the clergy, seems conspicuously cold and sad. But the empty chapels lying beyond it all about into the distance are a trap on sunny mornings for the clouds of yellow effulgence.

It seems to me that this is exactly how I experienced Canterbury Cathedral, and the school's part in its ceremonies, when I first went to services as a junior member of King's. After a term, having won my hoped-for scholarship, I would wear a surplice myself, and take part in the processions, the dignified bowings and scrapings, according to right.

Indeed, it doesn't do to underestimate the pleasure we all of us got from our place in the ritual. Not because many of us were particularly devout—the era of juvenile religiosity was already long over—but because of the sense of the fitness of things we got from it all. There was, for example, a minor but very definite satisfaction to be derived from taking part in the procession from the choir into the nave on one of the grander Feasts of the Church.

At Canterbury, the choir stands up, supported by the crypt, and a flight of stairs, with the nave altar at the bottom, leads from one to the other. Passing through the arch of the choir-screen, the procession therefore divided and moved down the steps in two lines, to come together again as we moved towards our seats. The difficulty was to rejoin one's appointed partner at precisely the right moment, having walked down the steps while out of sight of him. As we fell into step once more, we would greet each other with a little bow, and a faint, self-congratulatory smirk.

We felt, I think, that our expertise in these small matters entitled us to take some aspects of the religious life of Canterbury rather lightly. Unlike the boys from the choir-school, whom long custom permitted to read comic books and other light literature, concealed for decency's sake on the ledge within their stalls, until their turn came to sing again, we boys from the King's School were expected to look alert and listen to the sermon. Our favourite preacher was the Red Dean, Dr Hewlett Johnson, then at the head of the Chapter, and making regular headlines in the popular press. He would always treat us to an impassioned discourse about the benefits of life under Soviet rule. We especially relished his performances if the Archbishop of Canterbury, then Dr Fisher, was also present. From where we sat, it was easy to see the Archbishop's face. As soon as the Dean began, Dr Fisher would lean back and appear to sleep; but, as the sermon proceeded, one would see the expressions of disdain and distaste passing across his craggy countenance, like cloud shadows across a ploughed field, though all the while his eyes remained firmly closed.

The glorious setting of the Cathedral, and the intricacies of Chapter politics, made a striking contrast to the religious atmosphere I had been used to in Jamaica. The services I had attended every Sunday in prep school chapel had made little impression on me, except for some of the hymns, sung to a wheezy harmonium accompaniment. We sang all the old four-square favourites—the Church of England was, in Jamaica, decidedly Low in its inclinations, 'terribly Protty', as a vicar's son once said to me at University. Often we got into trouble by out-distancing the organist, a member of staff who liked to add syrupy decorations of her own to the unlikeliest melodies. We disapproved of these, because they slowed things down. Our Christian soldiers would be marching at a brisk military pace, while the accompaniment laboured along, almost a verse behind. These differences in musical opinion would bring us a scolding from the headmaster's wife, who rehearsed the hymn-singing on Saturday evenings. But on the whole she encouraged us to sing out, loudly and forthrightly. 'Don't scoop, boys!' she would cry, waving her baton. 'Don't scoop!'

The hymn-singing we liked best, in those Jamaican days, came when we were occasionally marched off to a joint Methodist-Church of England service, held at a chapel in the town. There we sometimes sang a hymn which was not in our school hymn-books. 'Dare to be a Daniel!' ran the opening lines, 'Dare to make it known!' The tune hit the words 'dare' and 'Daniel' with a tremendous thump. Its militant fervour comforted me in those sad days.

The dramatic change in setting, as in the hymns we sang, was another symbol, a more appropriate one than the conical hills of St Austell, of the change which was now overtaking my life. 'Dare to be a Daniel!' was somehow not an imaginable sentiment, either in the soaring choir of the cathedral or in its mysterious crypt, where school evensong was usually held. Now we sang modal melodies, often intricate, and the words we sang were frequently those of the seventeeth-century mystics, such as Vaughan and Traherne.

Looking back, I am still puzzled to decide how much these early religious influences meant to me, apart from the immediate play of emotion. I certainly cannot say that they made me into the practising Christian both my headmasters would have wished me to be. But they are still powerful enough to prevent me from writing the word 'agnostic' when asked to specify my religious tendency on some official form. The pen automatically traces the initials 'C of E'. And churches are still things I visit furtively, on summer holidays, telling myself that I am interested only in the architecture. What I like best are remote country churches, in parishes where the congregation has almost vanished. If the door is not locked against vandals, as increasingly happens nowadays, I creep in to savour the whiff of damp, of dying flowers and snuffed candles, without being able to say quite what it is that brings me here, or why churches of this sort seem to reflect my own state of mind.

By a further progression of thought, I begin to wonder, as I write these words, what Fred Shirley would have thought of my efforts. Not much, I suspect, though he might be pleased, though a little nervous, about my attempt to describe the school. Were he still alive, there would be many things about which we might differ.

Yet, like every boy who attended the King's School under the Shirley régime, I willingly admit that it was the man, even more than the surroundings, which moulded my school experience, and, in my case, made it so different from what I had endured in Jamaica.

Canon F. J. Shirley, or 'Fred', as he was universally called behind his back, may well turn out to have been the last of the line of 'great' headmasters who descended from Arnold. He would not, I think, have denied the histrionic streak in his own personality. Indeed, it is probable that he deliberately cultivated it, as an essential tool of his trade. On the other hand, he would not have been entirely pleased by the label 'fixer' which now, a generation later, would inevitably be attached to his character.

Fred—one should begin with the outside—looked a little like a prosperous farmer; and then, too, he looked like a rural clergyman of the mid-nineteenth century. He had silver hair, fierce eyebrows, a ruddy face, a wilful mouth, and a resonant clerical voice with a slight whine in it. His most conspicuous sartorial foible was a low-crowned, wide-brimmed black hat—a kind of mourning sombrero. If you looked at him more closely, you noticed that his shoes were always beautifully polished; it turned out that he polished them himself, with infinite care and skill. This little job was his daily release from tension.

He had come to King's in the thirties, from a previous head-mastership at Worksop. The school had then been nearly bank-rupt; Fred, when offered the job, had insisted on a canonry at Canterbury in case it collapsed altogether. But it had not col-lapsed. Instead, it had been saved, transformed by Fred's energy and cunning. He had seen it through the period of Cornish exile, and now that boys and masters had returned to their proper home, he had started to build it up. The process was to continue long after my time; the school as it now stands is, physically and in reputation, the product of the redoubtable Canon Shirley. The new buildings that surround the Mint Yard and the Green Court are his visible memorial.

Clergyman though he might be, Fred was a worldly man. The boys recognized the fact, and he himself seemed to relish this aspect of his own character. Once, later in my school career, I wrote the libretto of a pantomime, loosely based on the story of Dick Whittington. Fred was caricatured as the heroine's father. This surrogate delivered the hit number of the show, a patter song which began with the words:

> I'm a poor, bewildered Canon,
> Torn in half 'twixt God and Mammon,
> Ah! will no one pity me!

Seated in the middle of the front row, Fred roared with delighted laughter, as did the packed ranks of boys behind him. The only person offended was the headmaster's secretary, a terrier-like lady who greatly resembled the matron at my prep school. No joke against Canon Shirley could be a good joke so far as she was concerned.

In real life, I don't believe the conflict between God and Mammon troubled Fred very much. He had chosen his rôle, and his rôle was that of the manipulator. He manipulated the Chapter, the Headmasters' Conference, the staff, the parents and the boys. He had a gift for extracting money from the most unlikely people. He felt that any celebrity who had once been connected with the school should be prepared to help it now. Somerset Maugham was one of the most famous of our living Old Boys, and Fred set out to get him. In view, not only of Maugham's own character, but of the unhappiness the writer had suffered at King's, it seemed an unlikely enterprise. Somehow Fred overcame all obstacles. Maugham gave money for new buildings; he gave the school a group of his manuscripts, handsomely bound; he even came to see us.

I do not think that this visit was a real success. I can remember the famous novelist sitting, like an aged tortoise, in the midst of a ring of boys. We none of us could think what to say to him, and he, equally clearly, could not think what to say to us. His wrinkled neck settled further and further back into his over-large shirt-collar, while his lips wrenched downward in a grimace of discontent and disapproval. But there was no outburst, the cheques continued to come, and Fred remained delighted with his catch.

Another distinguished visitor who had also, as a small boy, had a brief connection with the school, was Field-Marshal Viscount Montgomery. In those days immediately following the war, Monty was a star of the first magnitude, and he seemed to be very conscious of his own charisma. His most conspicuous prop was his car, a dashing Rolls-Royce coupé, the product of some ultra-fashionable coach-builder of the middle 1930s. It had a V-shaped windscreen which, instead of sloping backwards, sloped forward like the prow of a boat, so that the roof of the car came to a sharp, aggressive point.

Monty's manner towards us was also aggressive, particularly when he addressed us, as he sometimes did, from the platform which had been erected in the cathedral Chapter House. On one of these occasions, he badly misjudged his audience. Arriving over an hour late—just as the kneelers had begun to fly over the heads of the assembly—he strode briskly to the centre of the stage and said, in his clipped soldierly tones, 'Boys, I'm not going to apologize for being late. Never apologize for anything—that's one of the things you learn in life. My car was held up by the traffic on the way down.' At this point his discourse was inter-rupted by a hastily suppressed burst of laughter. After that, his reputation with us was never high, though his presence on school speech-days might impress outsiders.

Courting people like Maugham and Montgomery was, how-ever, only one part of Fred's master-plan. Another part of it seemed to focus on the possibilities and potentialities of clever boys such as myself. It was often said that he collected potential scholarship winners with a passion other headmasters reserved for star athletes. Once corralled, we were beautifully taught, and I, for one, responded like a throughbred in training.

Yet, in describing Fred thus, I am conscious that I am being unfair to him. Not only was he a man of immense fascination, but he cared for his boys as people. He did not condescend. And he had a particular affection for the members of the awkward squad. Very rapidly, he and I developed what might almost be described as a friendship, if such a thing is genuinely possible between an extremely junior boy and the headmaster of a great public school. He fell into the habit of sending for me to come to his study, on the pretext that he wanted me to run some errand for him. The errand was seldom accomplished. I would arrive at his house—one of the large, comfortable houses which went with the various canonries—to find him working in the ground-floor room he used as a study. It was a pleasant room. It smelt strongly of the best beeswax furniture polish, and a number of superb Rowlandson drawings hung on the walls. Immediately I arrived, Fred would begin to talk, as if he had been keeping a torrent of words dammed up until my arrival. Taking me by the arm, he would walk me up and down the room (I can't remember that I was ever told to sit).

Though I recall the force and passion of these discourses, I can-not recall their content in any detail. One reason for this is that Fred did not stick to the point. His mind ranged, and so did his talk. He was constantly in search of information—about what was happening in the school, about one's reactions to his ideas, about one's own thoughts and feelings. He would stop in mid-flow, suddenly turn one towards him by the arm he was gripping, and poke one painfully in the midriff with outstretched forefinger, rather as if one were a chicken or a ripe melon, and he the housewife who was thinking of buying it. 'Isn't that so, m'dear?' he would say, or, 'Now what do you think, m'dear?' His strange, rather high-pitched pronunciation of the phrase 'my dear' was famous in the school, and constantly imitated.

Gradually I lost my terror of giving a straight answer. He did not mind—in some ways he rather liked—being contradicted by his boys, though he would not put up with insolence. It showed a spirit of independence, which was something he wanted to encourage. On the other hand, he did not at all like being contradicted by members of the staff, whom he regarded as being merely his appointed instruments. I have often wondered why he took so much trouble with me in particular. I think the answer is that Fred was essentially a romantic, but a romantic of a highly specialized kind. What thrilled him was the idea of potentiality. He had scented something in me, and he meant to get at it, to make it flower. Quite certainly, he was determined—as I only came to realize much later—that I should make a career as an author.

CHAPTER TEN

THE SUMMER OF 1946 had been a poor one. Now, as the autumn term began at Canterbury, the cold weather began to set in. A few weeks before school broke up, which is to say sometime in November, there was an unseasonable snowstorm. I watched the soft, wet flakes whirling down, the whiteness blanketing the grass of the Mint Yard, and ran out to scoop up some of its substance in my hands. I was thirteen, and it was the first time I had ever seen snow.

In London, that Christmas holiday, snow soon became familiar—a dirty grease clogging the pavements, a hard rime that made one's footing uncertain. We had all of us—my mother, a friend of hers, Paul, and I, moved into a vast rambling basement flat in Marylebone. Though the rooms were tall, they were entirely below ground. If you looked diagonally upward, through the sitting-room window, you could see booted feet, but only to the ankle, trotting by on the pavement outside. Gradually we abandoned room after room, since it was impossible to heat them. The last redoubt was my own bedroom, which had only a small stretch of outside wall, pierced by a tall, narrow window which looked into an equally narrow courtyard. Gloomy as it was, this room had an essential asset—a gas-fire which worked, even on the reduced gas-pressure available. The new ice-age had begun.

Back at school, warmth was even more difficult to achieve. East Kent is a notoriously cold area—it is often as cold, so the meteorologists tell us, as the east of Scotland. School rumour had it that Fred, years before, in one of his moments of cunning, had made a contract with the local supplier of electricity, upon somewhat special terms. The school was to get its current at a cheap rate, provided that, in an emergency, it would accept being the first to suffer cuts. The emergency had now come, and power immediately failed. Even after its restoration had been negotiated, it was not on very often. Power-cuts were a familiar misery all over the country.

In any case, the school buildings were hard to heat. School House, the boarding house where I had been placed, was a gaunt pile faced with knapped flints that looked like a Victorian rectory. Much of it, at ground-floor level, consisted of tiled corridors through which the draughts whistled. The heavy doors were equipped with garden-gate type latches which seldom caught properly if you slammed them. With eighty boys going in and out, these doors tended to hang open whatever the weather. Upstairs, some of the dormitories were immensely high. One, which had been designed as the school refectory, was a barn-like room with no ceiling. The peak of the roof must have been nearly thirty feet above floor level. As we went to bed, our breath hung in the air in steamy clouds. We piled all the clothes we had on top of our blankets, and still were cold. The weight of dampish wool —blankets, overcoats and dressing-gowns—piled on top of us made it difficult to turn in bed, and in the morning our bones ached.

At first, the school authorities tried to keep some semblance of normality. We sat in our classrooms wearing overcoats. Our frozen feet were encased in several pairs of socks, and then in Wellington boots. In spite of the cold, the wool and rubber made them sweat, and a faint, acrid stink gradually filled the room.

Even this poor version of ordinary school routine could not be maintained for long. It was too cold. In fact, it was colder in our dormitories, studies and classrooms than it was outside. There, at least, the sun often shone, striking the frozen puddles like steel on flint. Fred decreed that we must go for walks in order to keep warm. Grumbling, we bundled into yet more vests and sweaters, if we possessed them, and sallied out into the frozen hopfields and orchards.

Kent is a county with an intricate landscape, perhaps the most intricate in England. Everything is small-scale, portioned out, patterned. The apple-trees stand in their orchards like dancers about to begin a quadrille. Now this intricacy was transformed by the violent winter. In some places, lines of division were eradicated by the snowdrifts, so that hedgerows disappeared, and instead of a chequerboard of small fields one saw a great expanse of undulating white, marked here and there by the tracks of animals and birds. The season was so hard many birds died, and one often found them frozen in the waste, their snow-powdered feathers ruffling in the wind. In other places, ice-storms had sheathed the trees in crystal and broken down their branches, which trailed towards the ground. And now and then, under some overhang or ledge, which had preserved it, one found an old spider's web, its remaining spokes outlined and made visible by frost.

Through this landscape we proceeded in disorderly procession, like peasants in a winter scene by Breughel, moving stiffly because we were so much bundled up against the cold, sliding on the frozen puddles, pushing one another, throwing snowballs. It was our hands and feet that suffered most. As soon as we came in from these walks, many of us would rush into the washrooms, and turn the cold taps full on. The hot water, even if it had been running, would have been too harsh for the purpose we had in mind, which was to hold our hands under the jet until the blood began to circulate again. As one stripped off one's gloves, one would see that the flesh was white and waxy—if one pressed a fingertip against some resistant surface, such as the tiles of the washroom, the dent would remain in it for many minutes. Then gradually, painfully, circulation would return. The water, itself near freezing-point, seemed to be almost boiling. The hand blushed and throbbed, and one was tempted to snatch it away before the thawing out process was completed.

Since this was the first English winter I had endured, I felt the cold intensely. One symptom or by-product of this was that I felt hungry. At first I did not recognize the sensation for what it was: I have already said that I was an intolerably finicky eater throughout my Jamaican childhood, and the finickiness was made worse by the fact that I had no hunger pangs to spur me towards finishing what I had on my plate. But now I found that my strange new sensations could be assuaged with great slices of new bread, liberally smeared with peanut butter and Marmite. All these items were off-ration, though bread was to be rationed later.

A row of little shops straggled away from the Mint Yard Gate, lining a road that led out of the city towards the open country. At odd moments, I would slip out to buy yet another new loaf from one of the bakeries. Gradually, from being a conspicuously thin child, I became a fat one, with a voracious appetite.

Before the physical transformation was complete, the seasons had changed. The cold winter was followed by a brilliantly hot summer. The little shops were suddenly full of huge black Kentish cherries. By this time, I had made quite a number of friends in the school. One was an elegant, rather affected blond boy of my own age, but in another house, which meant that the friendship was frowned on. When summer came, we would slip away together as often as we could. Patrick had discovered the perfect goal for these expeditions. Our school playing-fields lay at some distance, on the edge of the town. Just behind the meadow that we used for organized games was a little ridge, once the site of a mansion which had later served as a convent. Now the big house had been pulled down, and a housing estate was going up where it had stood. Large parts of the grounds, now thickly over-grown, were still untouched by the developer, and it was these that we took for our own domain.

The path we most usually followed had once been a rhododendron alley—now the rank plants crowded so close that it was difficult to force a way through. Buried in the midst of them was a mausoleum, built when the big house belonged to the church. In part, it was built of the knapped flints so characteristic of the region, and in part of human bones, which were arranged in decorative patterns to form pilasters and quoins. A rusting iron gate, immovably locked, barred us from the dank cell which formed the interior, but straggling beams of light, slanting through the doorway, revealed disordered piles of skulls.

Beyond this, the path continued—to end, apparently, in a blank and crumbling wall. The wall, however, did have a few openings a little further round its circumference, though these were blocked with boards. Some of these boards had been pulled loose, and it was possible to force a way through. On the other side of the wall, a magic kingdom disclosed itself. Against it had been built a three-roomed garden pavilion, dating perhaps from the late eighteenth century, and now in a state of total dilapidation. The windows and doors had long since gone, the fine plaster ceilings drooped in long swathes towards the weeds which pushed their way through the rotten floorboards, and the roof had lost half its slates. Every time we went there the dereliction was worse: it was clear that, in addition to ourselves, boys from the town had discovered the spot, though no one ever interrupted us during the afternoons we spent there.

The garden pavilion faced a walled garden, which must once have been elaborately laid out—a dry, shallow, serpentine ditch indicated that there had been an artificial stream running through it; great patches of nettles seemed to mark the positions of dried-up ponds. There were apple-trees, long past giving fruit, with moss growing on their sickly branches. Butterflies—cabbage-whites and tortoise-shells—fluttered lazily about, and bumble-bees tumbled in and out of a few remaining flowers.

We always brought a picnic with us, and books. It seemed the perfect place for reading, and we tried to fit the literature to the atmosphere of the place—the diaries of Denton Welch, the poems of Edith Sitwell were frequently transported there. We seldom had to change our choice of books because, after glancing self-consciously at a few pages, we both of us, almost invariably, went to sleep. It was a sleep-inducing spot—though the innocent use we made of it would not, perhaps, have been believed by the school authorities.

Patrick also liked to go further afield. He was a great snob, and he had a passion for country houses. He often found it possible to indulge in both of these passions at once, and he found in me a willing accomplice. Kent abounds in manors and castles. On Saturday afternoons he and I would put on our best clothes (the school uniform of black coat and striped trousers, topped off with a wing collar), polish our shoes, sleek down our hair, and sally forth to do a little gatecrashing. Sometimes it was a matter of climbing into the grounds of a house which had long been shut up. I remember a splendid Regency villa, the blinds drawn, crocuses pushing their way up in the deserted gardens that surrounded it. I remember, too, a charming eighteenth-century gothic house, already in the hands of the wreckers, where we sat in the sun, using one of the massive traceried wooden window frames that the demolition contractor's men had wrenched from their sockets for a bench.

If the house we wanted to see was occupied, we walked up the drive to the front door and rang the bell. This impertinent boldness was often successful. We were shown round the house; we were given tea; sometimes we were even tipped.

The houses we liked best were Godmersham Park and Chilham Castle. Patrick's parents had, I think, some connection with the owners of Godmersham, a mid-Georgian house which had once belonged to a brother of Jane Austen. At a time when everything was shabby, run down, neglected, it was kept up with astonishing style—the window-frames were freshly painted, the gardens immaculate, a butler stood to receive you at the door. Within was fine Regency furniture, a set of Mortlake tapestries, and bookshelves full of first editions of the works of the great novelist. Gravely we inspected all these, gravely we replied to the polite questions put to us by our hosts. What I really liked, however, was the orangery, which had been turned into a luxurious sun-room, full of thirties-style bamboo furniture. It looked like a set for one of the riper comedies of Noël Coward. Godmersham itself seemed fixed in the epoch of Noël and Gertie; it had no intention of succumbing to post-war conditions.

Chilham Castle, a more famous house, was not so immaculate. Here we never succeeded in penetrating further than the hall, but we were allowed the run of the gardens, which fell in a series of terraces towards the bottom of the hill, on top of which the castle itself was perched. These terraces looked over a weed-choked lake, with a heronry. We would descend slowly towards this, and stand on the brink—the water looked up like a great eye towards a heaven full of greyish clouds, from which the light was fading in the summer afternoon. Far off, in the woods, a blackbird called. Nearer, a heron very slowly turned his head to look at us.

A third mansion that we sometimes visited was Broome Park, a Dutch-style house of the mid-seventeenth century which had once belonged to Lord Kitchener. I was mildly interested in it

because this celebrated and sexually ambiguous soldier had been
married to a distant relation of mine on my mother's side. Our
real reason for going there, I must admit, was not this tenuous
connection, but the fact that the place was now run as a private
hotel by a couple who had a son at the school. Patrick and I both
disliked this boy, a haughty, awkward creature with a well-
developed gift for making disagreeable remarks—looking back,
I realize of course that this was self-protective.

His parents were short of help to run their establishment, and
on Sundays Archie would often serve lunch to the guests. We
made a point of eating Sunday luncheon there from time to time,
though the food was little better than what we might have had
at school. Complacently settling ourselves at table, spreading our
napkins on our laps, we would wait for our enemy to shamble in,
a thumb in one of the plates of soup he carried at a perilous angle.
These plates he would slam down in front of us, then turn on his
heel without a word said. Nodding sadly to one another at this
display of gaucherie, we would pick up our spoons and begin to
eat.

CHAPTER ELEVEN

PATRICK WAS NOT the only close friend I made at school. Another was Wilfred, another of Fred's intellectual thoroughbreds, my exact contemporary and a member of my own house. Wilfred had flaming red hair and looked like a pocket edition of George Bernard Shaw. Though he had not as yet managed to grow the requisite beard, it was present, so to speak, in spirit. Wilfred only took a term or so to set himself up as the school Communist. His keenest pleasure was to confound boys and masters alike with quotations from *Das Kapital*. He soon became a great favourite with the Red Dean, and used to slip away to the Deanery for clandestine visits—we boys were forbidden, unofficially but quite firmly, to have anything to do with its occupant. Wilfred returned, full of buttered muffins and left-wing ardour, to give me vivid descriptions at second hand of life in Soviet Russia.

He fascinated me for two reasons—his self-confidence and his power of argument. He was physically extremely restless, and could only talk while on the move. I would follow him round the circumference of the Green Court while he expatiated on the injustices of the capitalist system or the shortcomings of the Attlee government, sawing his fist in the air to mark the points he was making. When not talking about politics, he liked to talk about the techniques of public speaking. He was constantly trying to instruct me in the various unfair tricks of the trade—the illogicalities and sudden transitions which could be used to keep an opponent on the hop. Occasionally, as we went into class, he would tell me to watch out for a particular trick he was going to try. If it succeeded, he would signal with his fingers and give me a triumphant look.

It never seemed to matter to Wilfred that people found his arguments difficult to answer rather than really convincing. When a mock-election was held, he stood as the Communist candidate, made by far the most polished oration, and received only three votes—one of which was his own. The Tory won in a canter. Wilfred was far from abashed by this, and maintained that it only showed the blinkered and repressive nature of the system under which we were living.

I was eventually to discover that his idealism could be tempered with self-interest. The moment came rather late in my school career. I was by this time editing the school magazine, an unusually lavish publication with spacious quarto pages. Fred allowed the joint editors to fill these with almost anything they liked. We decided, since it was very much the topic of the day, to do a piece on National Service—almost every boy then at King's could expect, as soon as he left, to do his time in the armed forces.

Our method of investigation was simple. We sent out a questionnaire to what we described as 'a representative selection of OKs'. Many of the questions were heavily slanted. For example, we asked, 'Would you now recommend a KS boy to join the School Corps? Why? What should the Corps try to do?' Other queries were included in the hope of eliciting anecdotes rather than straightforward information. Part II of the document began with the question, 'What were the first words your CSM said to you?'

The report we based on the answers returned to us is, I think, both informative and amusing. Some of the material is mildly thought-provoking even today. The answers revealed the time-wasting boredom of Army life, even though many of our respondents had achieved National Service commissions. One such young officer, stationed in England, described the way in which he was currently spending his time thus:

(a) gossip, yawning, drinking, laughing in the mess. (b) In second-hand bookshops. (c) In reading the *News of the World* on Sundays; A.C.1's, N.C.O.'s, D.R.O.'s Parts I, II and III, and Garrison Orders, Educational Directives, Re-Settlement Bulletins, and War Office ballyhoo from Monday to Friday, serious literature on Saturday. (*d*) Walking, satisfying the Colonel by brandishing a hockey-stick.

Another thing which emerged clearly from the answers given to our questions was the fact that National Service was not performing the rôle, claimed for it by Field-Marshal Montgomery in one of his rambling speeches to the assembled school, of breaking down the class-barriers in English life. One question read as follows: 'What are the professions, or prospective professions, of your three best army friends?' This was how we reported the answers:

The order of popularity was: Regular Army Officers by far the most, with six entries; next came four who intended to go on to the Universities, three schoolmasters, three engineers, two prospective psychologists, two undecided. One conscript was friendly with a West End tailor. On examining our results here, we at first felt inclined to say that friendship in the Army depended less on class than on intellectual level, but in view of the remarks on Regular Army mentality which appeared in the same question-sheets, we must leave the reader to judge.

The new issue of *The Cantuarian* was usually distributed to the boys a few days before the end of term. On the day this particular number became available, I saw Wilfred, who was usually scornful of our efforts, reading his own copy with great intentness. Later, I saw him in the telephone-box which stood just outside the Mint Yard gate.

The next morning the *Daily Express* had a sensational report of our survey and its results spread across its middle pages, under a variant of the old 'King and Country' headline. Fred received a number of letters of protest from Old Boys and parents, and we editors got into hot water as a result. Wilfred told me, with marked smugness, that he had more than doubled his pocket-money for the term because he had had the idea of making a phone-call to London.

Though Patrick and Wilfred both had a definite fascination for me—the one for his lazy elegance, the other for his energy and cleverness, there was no touch, with either, of sexual attraction. In fact, I never formed a 'particular friendship' during my time at King's, though such friendships were known to exist in the school. I was sexually rather reticent, and the manifestations of sexuality in my own body frightened me—though I joined in dormitory jokes and horseplay, such things as masturbation races under the sheets made me uncomfortable and embarrassed.

One night, when I had been moved to a dormitory which housed the fifteen- and sixteen-year-olds of the middle school, an occupant with a bed across the room from mine happened to glance out of the window behind him. This overlooked one of a row of working-men's cottages just beyond the school wall. In the nearest cottage the lights were on, the curtains had not been drawn, and a young couple could be seen vigorously copulating. Soon almost all the boys in the dormitory were crowded at the far windows, and the inventor of the spectacle was giving a running commentary on what was going on, in the style of a radio sports reporter. I alone refused to go and see for myself, though I listened intently to the description.

Just before this incident, I had had my first, and painful, experience of unrequited love. Doubly painful, because I was the party unable to respond. About two years after my arrival at King's there arrived, as part of the new intake, an outstandingly ugly boy with a Jewish name. I was not, and the school was not, anti-Semitic, but this child had the indefinable aura which attracts persecution. Having possessed this myself at my prep school, I was terrified of any contact with it—rather as if the capacity for suffering were a disease, which could be contracted again. Cohen (which is what I will call him here) seemed to sense my terror. He began to follow me round wherever I went, oblivious to any threats, apparently indifferent to insult. If I had been reading in the library, I would come down the steps that led to the Mint Yard and find him waiting for me. He always seemed to know when I was going to emerge.

Two terms went by, and Cohen became increasingly importunate. It was impossible to guess what he wanted. Indeed, it seems unlikely that he himself knew what the need was that only

I could fulfil. The thing which made him particularly frightening, so far as I was concerned, was the complete shamelessness of this unknown need. You only had to look at him to see it stirring in his eyes.

Just as the situation seemed to be moving towards some kind of climax, Cohen fell ill, and disappeared to the sanitarium. The next term, to my vast relief, he was gone altogether. I never dared to enquire into the reasons for his removal from the school.

In a more general sense, I remained rather dangerously interested in seducing my schoolmates. I wanted to be a centre of attention. In fulfilling this aim, the narrative skills I had acquired in Jamaica continued to stand me in good stead. My speciality was ghost-stories, the more violent the better. And from these it was an easy transition to experiments with the supernatural.

The place chosen for these experiments, which took place on a series of winter Sundays, was the room over the gateway which led from the Mint Yard into the Green Court. This room was used as an occasional classroom, and was furnished with desks and tables. It was ideally secluded: the only way of reaching it was through the school library, which was adjacent to the gateway tower. Approaching footsteps sounded loudly on the library floorboards, and louder still on the bare planks of the stairway which led upwards to the room itself.

On one of the tables we put a stack of foolscap paper. The method of communication was to be the simplest available —automatic writing. I had learned about this from a friend of my mother, who claimed to have mediumistic powers. Her own method was what she called 'psychometry'. Holding in her hand an object borrowed from one of the company, to serve as a form of conductor for psychic influences, she would launch forth into a long discourse. partly divinatory, in that she talked about incidents in the past which were presumably unknown to her, and partly hortatory and prophetic. Though she did not herself practise automatic writing, she was willing to explain, in some detail, how it was done.

Now, obedient to the instructions she had given me, I seated myself in a chair before the pile of paper, a pencil held loosely in my hand. The others, whom I had brought with me as witnesses (there were two or three of them) watched. The flat light of an early winter's afternoon came through the high window of the room and fell on the paper, where hand and pencil alike cast almost no shadow. As instructed by my mother's friend, I tried to 'make my mind a blank'.

Almost at once, my right arm was seized by a tremendous muscular spasm, and my hand began to rush across the paper. I was pressing so hard on the pencil that occasionally, during its rapid progress, it tore the sheet. As each sheet was completed, one of the witnesses pulled it away from beneath my hand, and I immediately began to write on another one.

When we looked at the scribbled sheets afterwards, deciphering the handwriting as best we could, a dramatic story emerged. A monk from the old cathedral monastery (the room in which we sat had once formed part of it) was denouncing King Henry VIII for the Dissolution. His vituperations were plentifully laced with Old Testament phrases.

Of course, we were thrilled. The experiment had been an outstanding success. We resolved to go on. And for two or three more Sunday afternoons, during that winter term, we did continue, with the same results.

By this time I was growing doubtful. I could not help noticing that the phrases used by the discontented spirit seemed to pop into my mind a split second before they appeared on the paper. Though my hand moved with such speed and violence that I suffered from cramps in the muscles of fingers and arm, I was nevertheless perfectly well aware of what I was writing. In addition, the monk soon became a trifle monotonous. He never seemed to enlarge his repertoire of denunciations, and was curiously unspecific about the details of his one-time existence.

The witnesses, who had been sceptical, were now enthusiastic converts. I was going in the opposite direction. More and more I began to feel that the monk was a figment of my own imagination, who had somehow or other managed to escape and embody himself upon the page, without my having full control over him. Rather than admit this, I looked for an excuse to stop the sessions. The spirit, I said, was so powerfully angry that I was afraid to remain linked to him. I insisted that I would have to give up, at least for the time being, in the interests of my own safety. And there the experiment lapsed.

Because this not very creditable episode stands at the very beginning of my career as a writer, it has since taken on symbolic implications for me. The perturbed spirit that I had half-consciously invented in order to impress my companions was an early manifestation of the demon that lies in wait for all the servants of literature—the demon of hysteria and self-indulgence. I am glad I got a glimpse of his true nature so early.

CHAPTER TWELVE

DURING ALL THIS time I had been passing examinations. One reason why I remember so little about my school work is that it gave me only minimal trouble. And it was not only that I enjoyed learning the things that were taught to me, I had blind confidence in my own luck. Stage-fright in the examination room was unknown to me, and I could never understand why others suffered from it. My freedom from tension was absolute —I was like a gambler riding a winning streak.

My gift for passing these tests soon promoted me into the upper reaches of the school. I moved out of the noisy common-room assigned to juniors, and into a study. And I began to accumulate quite a number of little distinctions and privileges. In spite of this, King's was really a less hierarchical school than most. Some of the senior boys, indeed, longed for it to be more so, and tried to impose new regulations. This attempt foundered on the stupidity of those who made it. A notice pinned on the main bulletin board started with the phrase: 'From today onwards it will be a school tradition that . . .' Instant tradition excited instant ridicule.

Nevertheless, there were such grave matters as the colour of the gown one wore, and the colour of one's hat band, and whether or not one was allowed to walk on the grass in the Green Court. These marks of distinction could be gained for either academic or athletic skills.

It would, perhaps, be logical to expect athletic prowess to have been the more fêted, and we certainly had our share of good athletes. Fred saw success at rugger, at cricket and on the river as a good way of advancing the reputation of the school, and exulted when we won an important match. But he was too shrewd, and, it must be said, too humane, to allow athletes to dominate the institution he had created. In a mild way, it was even fashionable to be clever at King's.

We senior boys were, indeed, extremely fashion-conscious. The dandyism which public schools encourage—one might almost say they are now the last refuge of the true dandy—was extended by us, and applied not only to manners and fashions of dress, but to the things of the mind. At sixteen and seventeen we took up and exaggerated the precious intellectual climate of the forties, in a way which might have surprised and embarrassed the founder-members of the *Horizon* circle. And we enjoyed, too, the rather more worldly atmosphere—as it seemed to us—which was to be found in the novels of Evelyn Waugh. *Brideshead Revisited* was the one which especially attracted us, not merely because it was lusher and more succulent than the rest, but because it painted, in its earlier chapters, the vision of an ideal Oxford. This vision dazzled us. Waugh's picture of university life in the twenties was superimposed by us, in our imaginations, upon the very different Oxbridge which awaited the more successful of us at the end of our school careers. Entry into this golden city, this ideal community, was the reward that awaited us when we flashed past the winning post, having triumphantly leapt the last of the many hurdles which the examiners put in our paths.

This may sound as if the tone of the school was rather precious, and it must be confessed that it was. There was a small, tightly organized élite, which spoke a special language, which giggled at private jokes, which found itself enormously amusing. I wish I could reproduce one or two specimens of this private language here, but I have forgotten nearly all of it. Its general characteristics would not, in any case, be particularly amenable to the medium of print. It was a matter of nuances, of the deliberate mispronunciation of certain words, of the overworking of certain adjectives. One of these adjectives, always uttered with arch emphasis, was the word 'tiny'. Things were a 'tiny shame' or a 'tiny bore', or else one was having a 'tiny difficulty' with some matter or other—a piece of French composition, perhaps.

Another, very important, element in this élite language was mimicry and burlesque. It was important to say certain things in a particular kind of voice—to use Fred's whining clerical accent at one moment, or to employ the flat moan characteristic of one of the English teachers at another. Perhaps because of the wealth of these linguistic tricks, our jargon never developed into something recognizable as a school slang. Efforts to preserve the school slang said to have been used in former times, and to promote its use, were ill-received by most of us, and provided yet another subject for ridicule.

Half-consciously, we used the jargon as a defence—and a defence at two levels. It protected the members of the club from outsiders, and served, not only as a mark of distinction, but also as a weapon against the school authorities. It is a little daunting to find moral drama so readily changed into farce, by a species of linguistic legerdemain. And at the same time we protected ourselves, through the convolutions of our invented manner of speech, from the realization of our own immaturity.

Not that we were by this time unaware of the more claustrophobic aspects of school life. The bolder ones among us were already experimenting in the woods and hedgerows with shopgirls picked up in the town. Others indulged in passionate male friendships, which seldom, I think, reached any form of physical consummation. Constitutionally reticent about physical things, I had found a different outlet, and was busy trying to turn myself into a writer.

I wrote my first poem, which was my first independent composition of any kind, when I was fourteen. I was spurred into writing it when a set of verses—uncommonly elegant and polished they were too—appeared in *The Cantuarian* over the signature of the detested Archie. Though I already relished many of the poems of Kipling, which I had discovered when reading those limp leather volumes, the model I chose for this initial effort was a very different writer: Alexander Pope.

I have sometimes wondered why Pope, in particular, attracted me so much. He is not supposed to be an adolescent taste. Yet I devoured his poetry, almost all of it, reading it in a sense which I now suppose to have been very different from that recommended by expert students of his work. The neatness of Pope's rhyming couplets made him only a step forward, from my own point of view, from the poetry of Kipling and Housman. In some poems, particularly *Windsor Forest*, Pope is a vividly pictorial, even sensual poet, but the sensuality is distanced by the literary conventions of his time (in this, he made a contrast with Keats, whose poetry I then disliked because I found it squashy). But, more important, he is a poet with a gift for the memorable phrase. In the *Oxford Dictionary of Quotations* he takes second place only to Shakespeare.

There is also another, more powerful reason why I liked Pope. He is a poet of unfulfilment, just as Kipling and Housman are. At my then stage of development, this was the kind of poet I wanted —one who did not threaten me with emotions larger or more complex than I could handle.

The poem I sat down to compose, as soon as I saw Archie's, was carefully tailored to reflect the ideas I then had about what a poem should be. Written in stiff couplets, resoundingly rhymed, it was about a mythical golden age. Here and there in it, randomly, like currants in a bun, were appropriate classical allusions. In no way did it resemble the kind of 'children's verse' which is now admired and publicized. It was extremely formal, totally impersonal, and perfectly unquaint. When I had finished, I was extremely proud of it. I thought I had produced a sound piece of craftsmanship. To some extent, at least, my admiration was shared by the then editors of the magazine, as they printed it in the next issue.

This little success was enough to set me off on a career as a schoolboy poet. I became, indeed, extremely conceited about my work. I can remember telling one of our English masters, about a year after my first poem appeared in print, that I intended to go down in history as the rival of the young Rimbaud and the young Blake. He blinked, but did not try to disillusion me. Blake's *Songs of Innocence* soon replaced Pope's translation of Homer as my chief model. Every issue of the school magazine now carried one or more little poems, and my prolific output led me to adopt several pseudonyms. Even for their extremely limited form, the poems lacked content. I still thought of myself as making something, a kind of verbal clockwork toy, rather than expressing something. To have admitted the need for expression would have meant admitting all kinds of other needs as well, and I was frightened of those.

I was now becoming fascinated with simple melodic effects. Even in my prep school days it had always been a frustration to me that I had no ear for music—the headmaster's wife, when she rehearsed our hymn-singing, constantly pounced on me for being flat. At King's, it was sometimes hinted that I would do better not to sing at all; it would be acceptable if I simply opened and shut my mouth, more or less in time to the music. I think I now felt that, by writing poems, I was at least making music upon the page, as a substitute for the music which was denied to me otherwise.

Soon enough, I had established myself as the school poet. Fred began to show me off to visiting lecturers, if these were literary. I basked in these attentions. It was only afterwards that I discovered that Fred had once described me as 'an example of the kind of boy who can survive in this school'.

Two established poets, who came to read their work to us, were kind with a kindness whose full extent I only now appreciate. John Betjeman, asked to peruse an immense stack of my work, including two rather uncharacteristic long poems in free verse, not only read my poems, but sat down and wrote me a letter which covered several pages. Its main theme was an admonishment not to abandon rhyme and rhythm. This was sufficiently flattering, but even more exciting things were to follow. Paul Dehn not only read my poems, but took a number away with him. Some weeks later, I received a letter from the offices of *Time & Tide*, enclosing a proof for correction. The guinea I got for this poem was the first money I earned by my pen. I was sixteen.

My long round of examinations had now left me with only one hurdle to jump—the examination for an Oxford scholarship. In one way, this test was less serious than the ones I had already passed; in another, it was more. It was less serious because it was already certain that I would go to a university. I had gained a State Scholarship in the examination for Higher Certificate, and a place would be found for me somewhere. But would that place be at either Oxford or Cambridge? In 1950, these two universities enjoyed a preponderance far more marked than is the case now. One reason for entering the scholarship examinations was that a boy who failed to gain an award might still hope to be offered a place by the College examining him, and, in that case, if he already possessed a State Scholarship, his problems were solved.

My situation, however, was a little different, and posed a number of ticklish problems. I had leaped the barriers so skilfully and traversed the course so rapidly that I had a year in hand. Fred was puzzled what to do with me. The thing he had his eye on was the brightest (at least to his mind) and the most glittering prize of all: a major scholarship at Balliol. On the other hand, the scholarship examinations for the Balliol group were not to be held until the autumn. Now, in the spring, it was the turn of a group of colleges headed by Merton. It was decided that I should be entered for this group 'to gain experience', but that there should be no nonsense about my accepting a place, or even a mere exhibition. I was to state on my form of application that I was willing to accept a major scholarship, and nothing else.

In due course I arrived in Oxford to sit the papers and to be interviewed. Merton is a quiet college, with the Meadow on one side, and on the other a cobbled street which discourages motorists. And Oxford out of term is often a melancholy place. The competitors assembled in the front quad, eyeing one another covertly, trying to work out the form, both social and intellectual. Later, we explored the undergraduate rooms which had been assigned to us, inch by inch, trying to imagine what it would be like to live here. The set which had been given to me were in the Rose Lane building, an addition Merton had completed just at the beginning of the war. All blond wood and folkweave, they offered little in the way of atmosphere, but they thrilled me all the same. Amongst the few books that the current occupant had left behind was a copy of Oscar Wilde's *The Importance of Being Earnest*. I had read it several times before, but now took it up again, as I liked the *idea* of myself reading Wilde in an Oxford college room.

On the free afternoon, before the examination began, I wandered out of Merton to take a look at Oxford itself. On a cold March day the town tended to look threadbare: Midlands industrial with a clump of sooty monuments in the middle, dank, unfriendly, forbidding. In the High Street, a small bookshop attracted my attention. If you concentrated on that, with a kind of tunnel vision, it all suddenly looked like the old Oxford of the prints—the prints one saw in the houses of distant relations. I looked under the beetlebrow of the window, and there, in the place of honour, was a small calf-bound book. The label beside it read *Charles I: Eikon Basiliké*. On impulse, I went in and asked the price. To my surprise, it was within reach of my limited amount of pocket-money. Since it seemed a suitable talisman for an aspiring historian to buy in Oxford, I took it away with me. The blond wood of the rooms in Rose Lane did not suit it, and I wondered afterwards why I had been so silly. It was only years later, long after I had lost or sold the little book, that I discovered that my father's ancestors had first arrived in the West Indies in the 1650s as Malignants—that is, irreconcilable opponents of Cromwell and the triumphant Commonwealth.

Of the papers set to us at Merton I remember nothing at all. I was so inured to the routine of taking examinations that I simply put my head down and wrote. My replies, I think, were super-ficial; they skittered across the surface of the subjects we had been asked to discuss. The interview was a more serious ordeal. The long wait before one went in to be cross-examined by the assembled Fellows allowed time for the collar to constrict one's neck, and for the palms of one's hands to begin to sweat.

On the other hand, I had already, with the help of a few allies discovered impromptu, begun to try to unsettle the other candi-dates. Most of them were so earnest, so desperately serious, and, after all, I had another chance. I had made a point, for example, of finishing one or two of the papers well ahead of time, so as to be able to walk out of the examination room with an ostentatious clatter. The agonized faces raised to look at me as I strode out, were ample compensation for any little rough places I might have left unpolished in my replies. Now, as I waited to be interviewed, the memory of these looks of anguish made me feel more cheerful.

I think the man who preceded me in the interviews must have

been an exceptionally dull candidate. At any rate, there was an atmosphere of deep gloom in the little lecture room as I was led into it. Hating boredom myself, I have always disliked it when people around me seem to be bored. Incongruously the impulse rose to put this slumped and sunken assemblage on the other side of the table into a better mood and a better frame of mind. All the specialized instincts which had turned me into the perfect classroom disciple now rose up in me. And a week or so later Fred summoned me to his study to tell me that a major scholarship at Merton was mine.

CHAPTER THIRTEEN

THE QUESTION NOW arose of what was to be done with me. I was only just seventeen. I could not go up to Oxford for more than a year—and my National Service commitment was in the process of being postponed until after I had taken my degree. At first, the decision was to leave me at King's. I idled away three whole terms in a state of delicious privileged dreaminess, steadily unlearning how to learn. But at the end of those three terms my mother rebelled. Fred wanted me to sit for Higher Certificate yet again, but she thought it would be more useful if I did something to polish up my languages. And so it was decided that I should spend a summer across the Channel.

Though excited by this, I was also regretful. Having arrived in England as the perfect outsider, I was now a contented insider. In those days, of course, one did not foresee that a public school education would in many ways be a handicap to a writer, and that it would be fatal to admit to having enjoyed it. Indeed, it was only very recently—I mean in the course of writing this book—that I found I could admit to having enjoyed it at all.

The journey to Paris was by rail and ferry. I loaded up a shabby suitcase made of real leather. My father had bought it in the 1920s, when no gentleman carried his own luggage. It weighed almost as much empty as it did full, and seemed to stretch one's arm to the length of an ape's. The train from Victoria was almost as battered and grubby as this venerable piece of baggage.

When we embarked on the ferry-boat, the weather was louring. The other passengers were, for the most part, nuns and school-girls—the former, presumably, in charge of the latter. The black robes and blue serge gym-slips gave the decks and saloons a gloomy air which matched the sombreness of the sky and of the sea.

As soon as the boat left the protection of the harbour, it began to pitch and roll irregularly in the Channel chop. The sound of falling teacups rang out between decks, and the stewards assumed that resolutely cheerful air which heralds a bad crossing. The nuns and the schoolgirls alike were soon prostrate and greenish. The worst-affected lay slumped full-length in the seaspray, or hung over the rails, their veils or mufflers flying. Altogether, this new phase of my life seemed to have got off to a bad start.

On the other side of the Channel, everything changed. The nuns and the schoogirls vanished. I lugged my suitcase across various sets of rails from the Customs shed, and climbed the high steps into the French carriage. As soon as I entered it, a feeling of happiness swept over me. A little later, sitting in the restaurant car as we glided through the green fields of Normandy, I fingered the edge of the tablecloth. It was stiffly starched, neatly darned here and there, but immaculately clean. The contrast with slovenly England was striking.

Equally striking, though anticipated, was the contrast between the meal I now ate (steak with a neat criss-cross pattern grilled on to it; crisp, dry *pommes frites*) and the British Railways food of the period. Greatly daring, I ordered half a litre of *vin ordinaire*, and savoured its acrid Algerian flavour on my tongue. Anything smoother would have been a let-down.

At the terminus in Paris, Mme Bonnemaison met me. She was to be my hostess, and, though I did not know it yet, the first of the series of female mentors who were subsequently to influence my life. Most of them, alas, lie outside the scope of this book. Mme Bonnemaison certainly made a striking contrast with the schoolmasters I had so recently left behind. She was shortish and rather broad in the beam. This breadth was accentuated by a frilled silk dress, the frills cross-banding her anatomy in complicated patterns. Her hair was red and frizzled, her chins were plural, her nose somewhat pendulous. By contrast, her legs were elegant and her feet conspicuously tiny. She was shod in simple black patent leather shoes with very high heels; and, as she advanced to meet me with little trotting steps, her chins and topknot shaking, she looked like a circus-pony with polished hooves. 'Ah, there you are!' she said, holding out a gloved hand which I duly shook. Something in her tone, and in the way she accented this ordinary phrase, gave it an air of wry humour. This humour, I soon discovered, was an important component in her personality. It was happily combined with an almost total pragmatism on all subjects. The God to whom Mme Bonnemaison appealed was the God of what was sensible. To a boy fresh from an English public school, this came as something of a shock.

Having met, we had a further brief journey to make together. Mme Bonnemaison lived, not in Paris itself, but in the adjacent town of St Germain-en-Laye, just saved from being a suburb by the castle, the woods and the great terrace which gave it an identity of its own. Boarding another train, Madame and I rattled towards it, crossing the Seine by a long, shaky bridge which still showed the effects of the war. The castle, part medieval and part Viollet-le-Duc, the latter perhaps predominating, faced a large reticent Jesuit church across the main square. Behind the church was a long street of elegant seventeenth-century houses, built, as she now told me, by the courtiers of Louis XIV, instructed by their king that one month in the year must be spent in paying their respects to the exiled James II of England, lodged somewhat uncomfortably in the *château*. Her own house, subtly different in pattern from the others in the street, had been built by the famous Duchesse de Longueville.

This dwelling sheltered a large household. Besides Madame herself, there were a son, a daughter, a grandchild and a son-in-law. And then there were the *pensionnaires*: a couple of English girls, a boy from Sweden, and myself. Finally, there was a poodle —a large beast the colour of stale milk-chocolate. He was called Tabu. So many people crowded under the same roof that there was no room for me. I was lodged in another house, immediately opposite.

I soon discovered that there were both advantages and disadvantages to this arrangement. The room allotted to me was on the second floor. One reached it via a steep, bare staircase, lit by bulbs as dim as glow worms. The lights worked on timers, set to the shortest possible span. The technique was to press the switch then sprint up or down the stairs as the case might be. The slightest hesitation meant being plunged in darkness. When this darkness descended, the smell which haunted the stairs was immediately accentuated, as if the nose was compelled to compensate for the insufficiency of the eyes.

But it was, in any case, an easy matter to trace this terrible odour to its source. All one had to do was to go to the ground floor and open a door tucked beneath the staircase itself. This action released an overpowering and by now unmistakable smell of excrement. The house was, apparently, constructed directly on top of a cess pit, and the toilet in this cubbyhole communicated, by means of a brief shaft, with the pit itself. There were no flushing arrangements of any kind—a wad of old newspaper was the sole concession to cleanliness. There was also no source of light. If you wanted to use the facilities, you took a torch with you. A single inspection was enough to convince me that bodily functions were better dealt with in the mansion across the road—the sanitation there, though of a somewhat ramshackle kind, had at least progressed as far as the age of the watercloset.

The room itself was almost filled by an immense brass bed. Any space left over was occupied by an equally enormous wardrobe. The mattress on the bed was conspicuously lumpy, and the lumps somehow suggested that they were monuments to the wars of sex, like the tumuli on some ancient battlefield. As it adapted itself during sleep to these excrescences, my body fell into strained erotic postures, as I would later discover on waking. Meanwhile, I was visited by extraordinary dreams, the more extraordinary, after the first few weeks, for being entirely in French. The moment of waking was always strange: the sprawling body to which I returned seemed that of a total stranger, something arranged in shapes till then unknown to me, the product of experiences other than my own.

The window was closed, not by curtains, but by metal shutters, pierced by narrow transverse slits. Through these shutters the clear morning light filtered; through them, too, came sounds which it was often difficult to recognize. A singing, swishing noise in the street outside suggested a downpour of rain, but, on flinging the shutters open, what I saw was a bicycle race—scores of bicycles, riders hunched over the handlebars, spokes glittering, careering past on the *pavé* below, momentarily filling the whole of the street, and filling the air, too, with the eerie noise of rubber on stone.

Despite the lumps in the bed and the smell on the stairs, I soon grew fond of that room. It was a place of refuge, a fortress into which I could withdraw when life grew too much for me in the Bonnemaison household. I would lie there in the afternoons, the shutters closed and the light on, reading the books that Madame had recommended. Despite, or perhaps because of, her pragmatic approach to life, she had romantic tastes in literature. St Exupéry's *Vol de Nuit* was one of her favourites, and another favourite was Montherlant's play *La Reine Morte*.

Any difficulties I found in the household were not due to Madame and her family, but to the other *pensionnaires*. The girls were daughters of the English upper middle-class, though it was in fact possible to make a firm distinction between them. Besides a marked difference in appearance, one being large and tawny, the other small and dark, it was immediately apparent that they came from different strata. Jane had more background than money, Mary more money than background. They competed fiercely, without apparently being conscious that they were doing so.

Having looked me over and found me unsympathetic, and having discarded Mme Bonnemaison's son in the same manner, they were left with only two possibilities. They veered in unison from one to the other. Their real favourite, and the object of their subtlest stratagems, was the son-in-law. It was he and his wife who had previously occupied the bed which was now mine across the road; indeed, I was soon given to understand that their baby had been conceived in it. The son-in-law had a glint in his eye; he also had great charm and looked, with his hollow cheeks, turned-up nose, and raven-black hair, like a French film star of the period. He well knew how to cope with the two young ladies—he flirted obediently, but always with a tinge of irony in his manner. In the end they found this discouraging, which was what he intended.

The two girls would then turn their attentions to the remaining guest, a hapless Swedish youth who gazed at both of them with moon-calf eyes. What protected him, to a certain extent, was the fact that he could never decide which girl he liked better. There was also a language difficulty. Although, like most Swedes, he spoke excellent English, their boarding-school slang and their exaggeratedly upper-class accents were sometimes too much for him, and he did not always understand what they said. Nevertheless, he would occasionally allow himself to be led away by one or the other. The girl who had been given the slip would fret openly until her rival came back, with the Swede still in tow. He, invariably, would look slightly shaken; she, rather smug.

Meanwhile, the son slouched about the house, occasionally trying to teach me a phrase or two of current teenage *argot*. Everything seemed to be either *vache* or *cloche* (both words meant 'disastrous'), and parents were referred to as *les croulants*. Tiring of this, he would take a disc from the stack of records—his own exclusive property, not to be touched by the rest of us—and the plaintive tones of Piaf, Trenet or Montand would fill the room.

Outside, in a percussive obbligato, a thunderstorm would rage —it was a bad summer for thunderstorms. Or else I would find myself discussing the finer points of English idiom with Madame and her daughter. We got into a terrible tangle, for instance, with the phrase 'Stockbroker's Tudor'. It seemed profoundly inadequate to render this as *le style normand*.

The best moments, the times when we were all in harmony, were meal-times. Living up to her name, Mme Bonnemaison kept an excellent table, in the traditional French style—the same knife and fork were used for each course, while vegetables were served separately from the main dish. Cheese preceded pudding.

Madame and her family were not ashamed to talk about food —not even when it was on the plate in front of them. We were expected to take part in these discussions, and to speak French when we did do. Any lapse into English would be greeted with a cry of '*Parlez français, s'il vous plaît!*' as Madame rapped the butt

end of her knife on the edge of her plate. Gradually these discussions educated me, not merely in French vocabulary, but in
the basic points of good cooking. One dish, a speciality of the
household, which I have never seen reproduced elsewhere, was
a kind of cream which was served once a week for dessert. It
seemed to be made of a mixture of fresh cream, sour cream,
sugar, and the finest and blandest cream cheese. With it came a
great bowl of ripe cherries, which we picked up by their stalks
and dipped into the mixture. The contrast with the conditions
that still prevailed in England could not have been more marked,
and Madame's cooking acquired a magical quality for this very
reason.

It soon became apparent, however, that French society was
paying a price for the quick return of good living. Constant
strikes interrupted the rail service that linked St Germain to Paris,
and there were occasional unexpected power cuts, in addition to
those caused by the thunderstorms. Whenever the conversation
turned to the war years, a tone of bitterness crept into it. Madame
told, I thought with a certain relish, stories of the barbarities perpetrated by the Germans towards the end of the Occupation.
One such story, which haunted me for years and gave me nightmares, concerned an old man who had had both his eyes put
out by the Gestapo, and who was then led on a circuit of
the town by one of his grandchildren, with eye-sockets still
bleeding.

Mostly, however, talk of the war turned into a discussion of
collaboration. Voices grew sharp as the Bonnemaisons listed
those who had collaborated and those who had not—writers,
actors, film-directors as well as politicians. Descending to the
world of personal and particular experience, hints were sometimes
dropped about the behaviour of certain of their neighbours
during the dark years just past.

The war was a topic which cropped up elsewhere, for example
at the Alliance Française in the Boulevard Raspail, where we
pensionnaires were supposed to attend classes every weekday. The
Alliance Française was organized like an ordinary French *lycée*
except that the pupils were all adults and all foreigners. The class
in which I was placed was conducted by a stern lady with a

moustache. Long years in the job had honed a characteristically French xenophobia. She corrected our mistakes in pronunciation with sadistic relish. The group over which she presided was able to produce a wide variety of different barbarisms for her to lash. Among us were to be found Americans, Arabs, Africans and Poles, in addition to a sprinkling of English, such as myself.

The Americans were studying on the GI Bill of Rights. They irritated our female dragon because they did not take her seriously. Indeed, they seemed to spend most of their time at the Alliance standing around in the courtyard, smoking Lucky Strikes and drinking Coca-Cola. I admired their studied casualness, the tight Yankee cut of their trousers, and the equally Yankee lope with which they walked.

The Poles, by contrast, were very desperately in earnest. They were refugees, studying to become Frenchmen, to make a new life for themselves after the chaos and suffering of the war. A bald, burly Polish ex-colonel suddenly rolled up the sleeve of his shirt to show me the concentration camp number tattooed on his arm. He smiled, showing ruined teeth, and in his thickly accented French tried to explain to me what it had really been like: the war, Poland, the winters, the camps he had been in. But before he had half-completed his explanation, the dragon swept in, and called the class to order.

I never had a chance to hear the rest of his narrative, because our attendance at the Alliance was very irregular. Mme Bonne-maison was always finding an excuse for us to skip school in favour of an exhibition or a visit to some museum we had not yet explored. We did all the standard tourist sights: the Mona Lisa, Notre-Dame, the Conciergerie. Madame, in the Grande Galerie at the Louvre, planted herself before Caravaggio's *Death of the Virgin*, and dismissed it abruptly as *art pompier*. In the Musée d'Art Moderne I took my first faltering steps towards an appreciation of contemporary painting. I did not get very far—in those days I still greatly preferred the late Derain to either Braque or Picasso. But I began to have a feeling that there might be some-thing in it.

As we went from one museum to the next, pausing occasionally for a cup of coffee or a *citron pressé* at some conveniently placed café, in order to rest Madame's feet, which suffered from her high heels and airless patent leather, I looked, and rather enviously, at the busy life of the Paris streets. In particular, the students fascinated me. I would see them in St Germain, then still in its first glory, or in Montparnasse as we made our way to the Cluny. Occasionally one would find them, always in couples, in the museums, entwined as they gazed at the pictures, each couple forming a kind of perambulating pretzel.

The fashions then were existentialist: the girls wore longish dresses in dark colours, and let their hair flow loose; the men had cropped hair and closely clipped chinstrap beards, and often, since the summer was hot, they wore shorts—in which case their costume would be completed by a pair of 'Roman sandals', a rubber sole, laced to the foot by a long thong, criss-crossed up to just above the bulge of the calf. For some reason, I became obsessed with this form of footgear, perhaps because it suggested a means of identifying with the students themselves. Using a couple of the pound notes my mother occasionally smuggled out to me, tightly rolled in copies of the *New Statesman*, I was at last able to buy a pair of these sandals in a Prix Unic—only to find, of course, that there was never any suitable occasion upon which to wear them.

Despite the Bonnemaisons' kindness, I began to chafe a little at the restricted life I was leading—the restrictions sprang from an almost total want of pocket-money, rather than from such regulations as were imposed upon me. For amusement, I was reduced to taking the poodle Tabu for long walks through the town, or along the immense terrace that flanked the castle.

Tabu was not an ideal companion on these excursions. Perpetually sex-starved, he insisted on making water at every corner, staining the stones with a thick oily stream of fluid. It seemed impossible that one canine bladder could contain such a quantity of urine. Tabu had other undesirable traits as well. When, as happened on hot days, we sunbathed in the garden, he would immediately try to straddle one or other of us. The only way of escaping his attentions was to use quantities of Ambre Solaire. He hated the smell, and would immediately flinch away as one

opened the bottle. The most effective punishment, if he mis-
behaved himself, was to sprinkle a drop or two on his coat. Poor
Tabu would rush round and round the house, trying to rid himself of the hated odour.

The tedium was occasionally relieved by a local celebration or
festival. The last of these was occasioned by the twenty-four-hour
race for small production cars, staged on the winding roads which
penetrated the Forêt de St Germain. The roar of engines drifted
with the wind right to the centre of the town. When we walked
down to the course, in the late afternoon, it was to find an almost
total absence of crash-barriers, or indeed of any attempt to control
the crowd. People strolled back and forth across the track just as
the fancy took them.

Their carelessness and lightheartedness were seemingly quite
unaffected by a tragedy which had taken place in the mid-
morning. A competitor had spun off the road at a sharp bend,
and had run down and killed the *gendarme* who happened to be
on duty there. The car, with no sign of damage, now stood
parked in the sunshine on the grass verge. Hooked over one of
the headlamps was a large funeral wreath made of marigolds, a
little like the wreaths which from time to time appeared under a
plaque fixed to a side wall of the big Jesuit church in the square
—this plaque marked the spot where two members of the Resistance had been shot by the Germans. The car and its adornment,
like the traditional skeleton at the feast, seemed only to sharpen
the prevailing mood of enjoyment. Four months in France had
made me feel almost at home there; now juvenile puritanism rose
to the surface and I felt more wholly alienated than at any time
since my arrival.

There was no time to get over the feeling. My allotted time
in France was at an end, and in a few days I recrossed the Channel.
I had reached the point when my tongue began to stumble when
I talked English. At the Customs shed in Folkestone, however, I
greeted English post-war surliness almost with relief. Curtly, the
official told me to open my case. His nose wrinkled when he saw
what was inside it. Knowing that I was soon to go home, I had
stopped sending clothes to the laundry, which was extremely expensive, and had tried to use such things as vests, underpants and

handkerchiefs as long as possible. The suitcase was packed to the brim with soiled, sour, sweaty garments. Meanwhile, the man next in line behind me was being hustled away for trying to smuggle a watch.

CHAPTER FOURTEEN

THE YEARS AT Oxford are well-trodden ground in English twentieth-century autobiographies. Or, if not the years at Oxford, then the years at Cambridge. People who write about themselves are quite likely to have attended one or the other. And, in a sense, the things they find to say about the experience are always the same. Until very recently, the two great universities remained the essential bridge to upper middle-class adulthood.

Despite this, I may have something to add to the accounts which have been given already. At any given moment Oxford undergraduate life has the tone of the time that is, and also of the time that is to come. The historic Oxford can speak for itself; what I should like to do here is to speak for an Oxford which is not yet historic in the full sense, but which is certainly no longer extant and actual. Mine, I think, was the last, or almost the last, undergraduate generation to pass through Oxford before the division opened between culture and youth-culture, overground and underground. It may be worth memorializing for that reason alone. I began my undergraduate career living one kind of student life, and ended it by living quite another. In the course of this piece of self-transformation I fell out with my college, but not with the ethos of the time.

I came up to begin my first term labouring under a disadvantage: I was two years younger than almost everybody else who came up at the same time. My contemporaries thus had a head start on me in the undergraduate career—and 'career' is a word which falls apropos when I think of the circumstances that then prevailed. The young men of the early fifties used the university as a stage upon which to act out fantasies of what their later lives would be like. Undergraduate politicians wore stiff collars, and were excessively political; undergraduate literary critics wore soft collars, and were self-consciously critical. The

world of amateur dramatics—the OUDS and the Experimental
Theatre Club—did its very best to reproduce the hothouse atmosphere of a London theatre which was then still dominated by
the big West End managements. All this led to a high degree of
specialization. You specialized not only academically, but in
everything you did.

Those who dissipated their energies could expect to be left
behind: you had to choose your race in order to win it, and not
try to run in several at the same time. Although my school
success had been to some extent founded on the competitive
instinct, I was not yet ready to attempt the choices which people
seemed to be making all around me.

At first, however, I was not aware of the contradictions and
tensions which were to mark my time at Oxford. I arrived on a
chilly October day, and found that I had been assigned a set of
rooms on the ground floor of Grove Building—a bleak, ugly
structure put up by Butterfield, and subsequently 'toned down'
to suit a less exuberant taste. The toning-down process, while
making the block less painfully conspicuous, had reduced it to a
kind of architectural nullity. Outside my sitting-room was a
lawn, and on the lawn stood a magnificent horse-chestnut tree.
In changing from bare branches to buds, and then to flowers and
leaves, and then again to bare branches, this was to be the clock of
my Oxford seasons, just as the Merton clock marked the divisions
of the day. Mob Quad and the college chapel were on the left as
you looked out of my rooms—the chapel itself out of sight, but
making its presence felt by the thunderous strokes of the bell.

Every college has its own character, not merely architecturally,
but as a social entity, though this second kind of character is open
to rapid processes of change. The Merton I knew as an undergraduate was tolerant in some ways, but much less so in others.
An immediate example of its tolerance was given to us newcomers when the Dean took us on a tour of the college premises.
Reaching the far corner of the grounds, just behind Grove
Building, he pointed to a place where the main wall abutted a low
railing. 'You will find, gentlemen,' he said, 'that this is the easiest
place to climb in. Please try not to trample on the flower bed. It
upsets the gardener.'

On the other hand, the college authorities were eager to have us understand that this was a place imbued with 'college spirit', one which maintained a difference between itself and the rest of the university. Traditionally, Merton has always held itself a little apart from the rest of Oxford—a Puritan part of a royalist whole. During the Civil War, the college had inclined towards the King's opponents, and the faint echo of that distant struggle remains. But in my day there were more immediate circumstances to account for this clannishness. Merton was setting itself up as a rival to Balliol, in terms of academic success. The scholars (Merton calls them postmasters) were shock troops in a battle which was being fought out in terms of alphas, betas and gammas. Secondly, 'college spirit' manifested itself in a different way —through the boat-club, the then Warden's pride and joy. Members of the club were royally treated: a special table was set aside for them in hall, and extra food was served to them—no small favour, at a time when rationing still prevailed.

My most immediate clash with the doctrine of 'college spirit' was with members of the club, towards the end of my second term. I had already attracted a certain amount of attention to myself as the college aesthete: the most conspicuous sign of my aestheticism being, perhaps, that I had changed my standard-issue college curtains for something gaudier. On an evening of boat-club celebration, my ground-floor rooms were a conspicuous and tempting target. In any case, it had been hinted to me that they might be the object of an attack. The new recruits to the boat-club—my own contemporaries at college—were, it seemed, looking for a means of asserting themselves as 'hearties', just as I was trying out a new identity as a languid young man.

That night, as the sounds of revelry grew louder and nearer, I prudently abandoned my rooms, and went to have coffee with a friend who lived in a different quadrangle. I did not really believe that much would happen if the revellers arrived and found me absent. Alcohol made them bolder than I had calculated. A small band burst open the door, and scattered my furniture over the lawns. Later, I returned to inspect the mess, and was not pleased with what I saw.

There were already a few signs of panic. An emissary, rather less drunk than the rest, was sent to find me, and see how I was taking it. I looked him up and down and said that, as far as I was concerned, everything was going to be left exactly as it was, and that I was now on my way out of college to take rooms at the George, where I intended to spend the night. This deliberate absence would certainly mean an enquiry, as we were not, if resident, allowed to sleep out of college during term. The emissary began to look a little troubled, and departed.

Soon enough he returned, this time with a message from the president of the boat-club. If everything was at least returned to my rooms, would I reconsider? I agreed to this, and the moving back process began. A light rain was falling, and the celebrants looked almost sober and distinctly sheepish. I presided over their labours with as blank a face as I could manage, meanwhile wondering if the lesson would serve its purpose. Apparently it had. Next morning I received a written apology. Feeling by this time rather guilty at the thoroughness of my victory, I agreed to let bygones be bygones.

I was less successful in dealing with the college authorities. As we headed towards the Preliminary Examination at the end of my second term, I was already beginning to resent the pressure my tutors put on me to justify my position as a major scholar. It was sometimes implied to me that the college felt it had bought a first-class degree, and that I was going back on the bargain if I failed to supply it.

The Preliminary Examination, and the summer term that followed it, marked a turning-point in my time at Oxford. I did well in prelims., with one notable exception. The piece given us to translate from Latin was a passage from Sallust, describing the Jurgurthan War. I had allowed my Latin to grow rusty during my idle last terms at school, and had taken no pains to repolish it since. I produced a translation which bore little relationship to the original. It was the first lapse in the luck which had stayed with me through so many examinations. I passed the examination as a whole, but the failure was noted at Merton. The *spécialité de la maison* was the history of the early Middle Ages. The special subject offered to the examiners by most Merton historians was the life and times of St Augustine, with his *Confessions* as the set text. For this, fluent Latin was required. It was decided that I was not up to it: I must do something else.

Faced with the decision, at first I protested, chiefly because I objected to having the choice made for me. But there was a strong temptation not to press the issue too hard. If I opted for some other special subject, I should be tutored outside. Careless of the fact that I knew no Italian whatsoever, I opted for the Italian Renaissance. Surprisingly, my option was accepted.

At the same time I began to venture outside Merton socially. My first experiment was perhaps unfortunate. In the first term of my second year, I allowed myself to be recruited for a production of *Julius Caesar*, which was being planned by the Experimental Theatre Club.

The rôle assigned to me was, at first sight, not onerous. I was to be an extra—flitting across the stage in a toga, and, later, wielding a property sword. This sword as I soon discovered, was by no means innocuous, nor were those issued to my fellow extras, most of them larger and brawnier than I. And we all of us wielded our weapons with a will, as the undergraduate producer had decided on a violent, hysterical presentation of the play.

The producer's ambitions, and his commitment to the task, soon brought me into conflict with the Merton authorities. Strenuous attempts were made to get me to resign from the production. As rehearsals proceeded, and I arrived heavy-eyed, and with increasingly sketchy essays, at my twice-weekly tutorials, the warnings I was given became ever sterner. Pressed from all sides, I became stubborn and incapable of compromise.

By this time, my involvement in the production itself was almost purely masochistic. I had two big moments, both of them mildly uncomfortable, one of them dangerous. In the early scenes I was cast as a decadent senator, a personage from the court of Elagabalus, rather than from the Rome of the last years of the Republic. I had devised, to compensate for my lack of lines, a fantastic make-up, with my hair combed into two horns, and fixed with lacquer. This at least drew an appreciative titter from the audience on our opening night. My big moment in the first half of the play came when I collapsed in a drunken stupor at Caesar's house—a scene which is generally presented as a quiet colloquy was here done as the aftermath of an orgy. The actor playing Caesar then proceeded to rant out the 'For I am constant as the northern star' speech while straddling my supine body. Often, in the excitement of the moment, he would trample on me painfully.

In the second half of the play, I was stripped of my senatorial adornments, and played a common soldier with the rest. The battle-scenes involved a series of tremendous charges along the aisles of the hall where the production was presented, and then hand-to-hand fighting on a series of high, narrow rostrums, shield pressed against shield. I, of course, was on the losing side; and, after tumbling from one rostrum to another, I was finally dragged off stage by one of my comrades. In the mêlée surrounding me, it was far more perilous to play a corpse than a live soldier, and I was lucky not to be hurt in good earnest. As it was, I accumulated, if not the battle-scars of a Roman veteran, then a collection of livid bruises.

After a full term of rehearsals, *Caesar* was finally presented to the undergraduate public, and to a few London critics as well. Harold Hobson pleased the producer greatly by saying, in a brief review, that it was the first Shakespearean production he had attended which seemed to put, not only the actors, but even the audience, in a state of physical peril. Reading this, I felt it was in some way an oblique tribute to my own efforts. Drunk with excitement and fatigue, we continued playing, to diminishing audiences, to the end of our planned week's run.

One question remained: Where were we going to hold the cast party? Very few of the cast had rooms in college, for most were already in their final year. Those who did have rooms were reluctant to offer the use of them, as the parties held at the conclusion of undergraduate productions were notoriously the wildest in Oxford. As it happened, I was in a position to help if I chose to. At the start of the new academic year I had acquired new and splendid rooms in the Fellows' Quad at Merton. These I shared with a fellow historian of the same year. With his consent, and in a spirit of defiance, I offered to house the celebration. My official request for permission to give a cocktail party was, surprisingly enough, agreed. Since few large parties were given in Merton, the college authorities may not have known what they were in for.

As the party warmed up, I grew anxious. And after a very little while, I found I was getting bored with the company of my fellow thespians. We had lived together for most of a term, and I had seen enough of them. Slipping away from the uproar, I went down the staircase and into the quadrangle for a breath of fresh air. From here, the celebration could be heard as a kind of animal roar, punctuated by drunken yells and screeches. As I stood there, looking up at my own lighted windows, I was suddenly confronted by the college Dean, drawn out of his rooms to see what the noise was about. Finding me there, he gave me a startled look. It was only after a long moment that I realized why he was staring at me so strangely. In my hand, I held the long-stemmed silver cup I had been drinking from—I had removed it from the mantlepiece as a precaution against its being purloined by an especially drunken guest. Askew on my head was the silver wreath which Caesar had worn as part of his costume, and which I had awarded myself as a souvenir. As my eyes locked with the Dean's, I recognized that my relationship with the college authorities would henceforth be distant, if not hostile. I had proclaimed myself to be an eccentric of the wrong sort—the kind of which nuisances, rather than legends, are made.

CHAPTER FIFTEEN

In the terms that followed, I at least found my feet socially in Oxford. My friends, however, were not a homogeneous band. They existed in groups, for the most part widely separated from one another.

In the first place, there were my college friends: despite my lack of college spirit, I had managed to discover a number of kindred souls. Our shared occupations were almost entirely frivolous, a continuation of the cliquishness of sixth-form life at school. We sat together in Hall, and played elaborate verbal games. A particularly apt repartee would bring a cry of 'Points!', and the number scored would be added up at the end of the meal. We needed something to distract our attention from the food which was, at that period, the worst in Oxford. We dared not complain about its unpalatability too much, because Merton was also the cheapest of the old-established colleges. A famous college character, Bursar Gill, still in office after many years' service, had devoted his life to husbanding Merton's considerable resources, and to employing them in such a way that the 'poor scholar' received the uttermost value for his college dues. If this meant very little plumbing and watery cabbage, we were compensated for this by the low battels we were asked to pay.

In common with a group of Mertonians of my year, I developed a passion for punting at night. We would wait until the College was quiet, then slip out and go down to Magdalen Bridge. Though the punt-hirer had long since shut up shop, it was not too difficult to pick one's way across the fleet of punts he had left tied up, ready for the next morning's customers, and to detach one from the outermost rim of the group. We would then set off up the Cherwell, and would explore all the byways usually considered impassable, dragging the boat over weirs and barriers where we had to.

These silent byways were exceedingly beautiful in the moon-light—the black water was dappled with patches of brightness, and such patches were textured by the fallen leaves and strands of weed floating just beneath the surface. Occasionally, we would reach a point where the stream was crossed by a pipe or a small footbridge. The punt itself could be forced under these barriers, but we ourselves had to swing across the obstacle at the same time, jumping from the bow of the boat, and landing again in the stern. Yet I do not recall that anyone fell in, even the man with the pole, who had a more difficult task than the rest.

During the summer term of my second year, I also often took a punt out during more conventional hours. I had discovered that it was the perfect sport for the unathletic, as one's progress through the water depended upon cunning, rather than upon brute strength. The slightest pressure on the pole sufficed to keep the boat gliding smoothly along, once a certain momentum had been attained. In fact, it was important not to exert oneself too much, especially on those stretches where the bottom was soft, as too much enthusiasm could lead very swiftly indeed to catastrophe. I was never left clinging to a pole fixed immovably in the river-bed while the punt glided away from under my feet, but I often enough saw it happen to other people. Punting is a traditional sport, in the sense that it sometimes corresponds very closely indeed to the images of it presented by old-fashioned picture postcards.

One of the delights of punting is that it can be either a social or a solitary occupation, and both give equal satisfaction. Punting alone, one is more conscious of the rhythm of the boat and the stream, and the corresponding rhythm of one's own gestures —dropping the pole into the water, thrusting, straightening up again, and meanwhile keeping the punt on the chosen course by varying the angle of entry, or even by pressing the pole for a moment against the side of the boat.

If alone, I would turn the nose of the punt upstream in the early afternoon, and continue my course until I reached a group of small, marshy islets, covered with clumps of sapling willow-trees. I would run the boat under one of the largest and sturdiest of these trees, and tie up, thrusting the pole down hard on the streamward side in order to keep the punt pressed steadily against the bank.

In theory, it was an ideal place to read, and I always brought some heavy tome with me, as a token of virtue. Usually, the intention to read and to make notes on what I read remained no more than that, as my island refuge was also a perfect place to sleep. After I had turned a few pages, my eyelids would grow leaden, and I would slip into a doze which lasted until the sun was off the water.

Just as often, I would share the punt with friends. If we had had any time to pre-plan the expedition, we would carry an elegant picnic with us, trailing a bottle of wine behind the boat at the end of a piece of string. Conscious of the twenties atmosphere of these jaunts—Waugh's *Brideshead* continued to exert its spell—we dressed in our best, the men in blazers and white shirts, the girls in filmy dresses, and would occasionally take with us an old wind-up gramophone. The tinny strains of pre-war foxtrots rang out across the water meadows to mark our progress.

Once or twice, feeling particularly energetic, we took a punt on an all-day expedition, going downriver to the Eights Week boat-race course, and thence, via a lock, on to the broad expanse of the Thames as it flowed towards London. Though the bottom, here, was hard and gravelly, punting called for a certain degree of skill—the flow of the current was stronger, and sometimes we bobbed uncomfortably in the wake of passing motor-boats. We would lunch on bread and cheese at a pub by a second set of locks, and then turn for home.

The journey back was arduous, as we were now making our way against the stream, and the long summer day waned as we crawled towards Oxford, taking the pole turn by turn. The breeze which sprang up as the sun sank in the sky played pleasantly against the sweat-soaked shirts which now clung to our chests and backs, and the slowness and effort of the journey gave us a ridiculous feeling of achievement when Magdalen Bridge at last came in sight.

If the memory of college friendships and college pursuits reminds me of how little Oxford seems to have changed when I go back there, the recollection of the friends I made, and of the

things I did, outside the Merton orbit, is enough to tell me that
in many respects the changes have been radical in the brief span
of twenty years. Two decades is, of course, an awkward interval
in terms of historical perspective, and this must be my excuse if
I judge the Oxford of the early nineteen-fifties rather harshly.

The careerism of undergraduate life was never more evident
than among undergraduate politicians at this time. The decline
of the Union was still to come. In the early fifties it retained much
of its old glamour. Ambitious would-be politicians still looked
with longing at what it had to offer: elections were fiercely con-
tested, because office at the Union, and especially the Presidency,
was regarded as a stepping-stone to Parliament itself. And certainly a number of our current MPs who were once my Oxford
contemporaries were holders of Union office.

I attended the Union assiduously, because the mechanisms of
politics had begun to fascinate me. It is, indeed, a fascination I
keep to this day. I soon discovered that I was not nearly as good a
speaker as I had supposed myself to be at school. My appearances
as a speaker—late at night, and for the statutory three minutes—
were not humiliating. No untoward disaster occurred. On the
other hand, it was plain enough that they made no impression
whatever, either on those who might be in a position to offer me
a so-called 'paper speech' or on the small and somnolent remnant
who remained to hear the rest of the debate after that night's
pride of lions had roared their best and departed.

Years later, I was at last invited to make a major speech in a
Union debate, playing a supporting rôle to two disc-jockeys and
a television producer. Even I could hardly construe this as a case
of long-overdue justice being done to my oratorical talents.
Rather, I took it as a sign of how much both Oxford and I had
changed in the intervening period. The subject of the evening was
Pop, and we had all been asked to take part as presumed experts.

Soon frustrated in my ambitions as a speaker, I took more
pleasure in the society of the Union bar than I did in the debates
themselves. A large part of the company could hardly be categorized as political—many found it a convenient watering trough
and a few used it, in addition, as a hunting ground. A senior
member of the University, famous for his scholarly editions of

the Romantic poets, would be seen, on debate nights, doggedly pursuing whoever was the handsomest male in the room. The blind persistence of his progress used to fascinate me, as he moved through the throng almost without seeming to notice it, as a porpoise plunges through the waves, his eyes unwaveringly fixed on the current object of his admiration.

Nevertheless, those with political interests and instincts tended to congregate at the Union rather than elsewhere. Here were to be found, at least on occasion, the stars of an epoch which was already over. The most gifted of these, and also the one who re-appeared the most frequently, was Jeremy Thorpe, who often held court in one corner of the room, sprinkling an otherwise serious discourse with repartees almost as brilliant as those he produced in the debating hall, where he was still a frequent guest-speaker. In conversation, as in debate, he seemed to thrive upon interruption.

The politicians who were my contemporaries seemed to me then, and seem to me now (though for quite different reasons) much less impressive, as well as less entertaining, figures. Quite a number of them are, or have been, Members of Parliament, and one or two have even held ministerial office. They include Michael Heseltine, Norman St John-Stevas, Gerald Kaufman, Ernle Money, Robin Maxwell-Hyslop and Peter Tapsell. I doubt if any of these would have the hubris to claim that they have played any major part as yet on the political scene, and I would venture to add that few, if any, are likely to.

Oxford atmospheres, while they last, can be both powerful and pervasive. Even in the political circles I chiefly frequented —which were Bevanite or left-Labour in complexion—the new radicalism, or even the politics of the New Left, had yet to come in. To an astonishing extent we accepted the world as it was, and no part of it more complacently than the undergraduate society we inhabited. Though we talked, for form's sake, about political issues, they did not, I believe, move us, as they were soon to move those only a little younger than ourselves. More than this, we never considered the politics of our immediate situation. An agitation like the one which is going on in Oxford as I write this, involving confrontations, either violent or legal, with the uni-

versity authorities, would have been unthinkable in my generation. As for a 'students' union', we were content to leave even the
idea of such an organization to the less privileged at red-brick
universities.

What interested us, in the outside world and therefore in the
microcosm of the university, was power—but power defined in
a peculiarly narrow way, the appearance of power, rather than
its substance. The world of undergraduate politics, at this time,
was notoriously corrupt. Every new round of elections in the
political clubs meant a fresh set of scandals, new subjects for
gleeful gossip about who had out-manœuvred whom, and
almost every election would be followed by a committee of investigation, where malpractices were righteously exposed.

It was matters such as these which formed the main topic of
conversation in the Union bar. On the nights when debates were
held the room would gradually fill up as the evening progressed,
with a sudden surge of latecomers when the main speeches had
come to a close. But it was those who remained in the bar
throughout the night's proceedings who regarded themselves as
the real connoisseurs, the string-pullers of the little world of
Oxford politics.

Another circle which I frequented was that of literary undergraduates. In retrospect, this was a better choice than the world of
undergraduate politicians. The Oxford of those days produced
its share of literary editors—among them John Gross, currently
in charge of the *Times Literary Supplement*, and Anthony Thwaite,
a co-editor of *Encounter*. Both of these graduated to their present
posts via the literary editorship of the *New Statesman*. More
strikingly, it produced a large number of poets who have since
made a name for themselves, among them George MacBeth,
Anthony Thwaite, Geoffrey Hill, Alan Brownjohn and Adrian
Mitchell. Indeed, when I now turn the pages of the magazines
and anthologies in which my own work appeared, side by side
with that of the writers whom I have just named, I am surprised
to note how many of us are writing still. The proportion of
survivors is, for example, much higher than the proportion of
poetical survivors to be found in the pages of the undergraduate
anthologies where W. H. Auden published his earliest work.

This said, I cannot claim that my undergraduate generation produced a poet as good as Auden, nor even one as attractive as Louis MacNeice. Changes were certainly afoot during the time when we were learning the poet's trade, but, looking back, they seem to me to be changes of rather a strange kind. Despite all the differences of temperament to be found among us, and despite the very different ways in which our work had developed in the course of twenty and more years, we began, it must now be admitted, as the heirs to a counter-revolution. Nor were we in the least reluctant to receive the heritage.

The counter-revolution was that curious affair 'the Movement', which was the creation of men considerably older than ourselves—Philip Larkin, Donald Davie, Kingsley Amis and Robert Conquest chief among them. The 'Movement' poets had a harder time in getting a hearing than is now commonly realized. Larkin had published his first book of verse, *The North Ship*, as early as 1945, but it was both a false step (from the point of view of his future development as a poet) and very little noticed at the time. Conquest's anthology, *New Lines*, with which the Movement celebrated its triumph, was not published until 1955, the year after I went down from Oxford.

But it has to be remembered that *New Lines* is a confirmatory rather than a revolutionary anthology. The counter-revolution had been made during the preceding five years, which was the epoch during which both I and my contemporaries (young poets at Cambridge as well as at Oxford) were trying to learn our trade.

There were many reasons why the new poetry should attract us—not the least of which was the fact that it was new, a secret knowledge, or (to change the metaphor) a club to brandish in the faces of our elders. We, like the undergraduate politicians I have described, were highly competitive, but competitive in an extremely conventional way.

Even so, what Larkin and his colleagues had invented fitted our own situation very precisely. It was, for one thing, a poetry founded upon the tradition of academic English studies—and many of us, of course, were reading English. Books such as I. A. Richards's *Principles of Literary Criticism* and his *Practical Criticism*, and William Empson's *Seven Types of Ambiguity*, were already

familiar to us, and the new manner in verse was in part a response
to the ideas put forward by these critics. When Donald Davie
published *Purity of Diction in English Verse* in 1952 he was consciously providing the poetry then being written by himself and
the other Movement poets with a rationale, and at the same time
following in the footsteps of men such as Richards and Empson.

We are saying [Davie declares on an early page of this volume],
that the poet who undertakes to preserve or refine a poetic
diction is writing in a web of responsibilities. He is responsible
to past masters for conserving the genres and the decorum
which they have evolved. He is responsible to the persons or
the themes on which he writes, in order to maintain a con-
sistent tone or point of view in his dealings with them. He is
responsible to the community in which he writes, for purifying
and correcting the spoken language. And of course he is responsible, as all poets are, to his readers; he has to give them
pleasure, and also, directly or indirectly, instructions in proper
conduct.

This is a slightly priggish programme, and that, I dare say, was
at least part of why it appealed to us.

In a more immediate fashion, the new poetry appealed because
of the people who approved of it. Now that the literary weeklies
have lost so much of their influence, as well as so large a part of
their circulations, it is sometimes hard to remember just how
eagerly they were read in the fifties, and especially by beginning
writers like ourselves. I lived for a long time at Oxford on the
renown of having had a poem printed in *Time & Tide* when I
was a schoolboy. At this moment, the Movement poets, previously ignored or despised, began to receive the support of a few
influential reviewers, most notably that of G. S. Fraser, who was
then principal poetry reviewer for the *New Statesman*. He spoke
approvingly of 'a new Augustanism in verse', and asserted that,
in comparison to the work of other contemporary poets, the
poems to be found in John Wain's *Mixed Feelings* has 'a kind of
masculine tautness of intellect'. Later, he was to say of Amis's
first book of verse, *A Frame of Mind*, published early in 1954, that

it offered 'an example of work in which positive values are, somehow, smuggled into brisk explosions of destructive statement'. These were the signals which we needed, to follow in the wake of the original Movement writers.

For some of us, it was the content of their work, as much as its style and its academic background, which seemed seductive. It was a portion of Larkin's originality that, while adopting conservative techniques of verse-writing, he articulated feelings and portrayed circumstances which were different from those which had appeared in poetry before. One of the strongest of these feelings was that of being excluded from somewhere or something:

> The trumpet's voice, loud and authoritative,
> Draws me a moment to the lighted glass
> To watch the dancers—all under twenty-five—
> Shifting intently, face to flushed face,
> Solemnly upon the beat of happiness.

We ourselves were still under twenty-five, but we thought we knew the emotion. And the same was true of the feelings of exclusion which played so large a part in some of Donald Davie's early poems:

> Those Cambridge generations, Russell's, Keynes' . . .
> And mine? Oh mine was Wittgenstein's, no doubt;
> Sweet pastoral, too, when some-one else explains,
> Although my memories leave the eclogues out.

Undergraduate poets, perhaps more consciously than other undergraduates, were subject to the stresses and strains which were undermining the seemingly bland Oxford of the time. We liked Larkin, in particular (though we would have died rather than admit this), because he found a poetic voice for those in the painful process of transforming themselves from *petits bourgeois* to *hauts bourgeois*—the situation of almost every undergraduate who had arrived to take possession of the gleaming towers of learning thanks to a State Scholarship.

One of my reasons for discussing the Oxford poetry of the time at such length—quite apart from my own passionate involvement with it—is that it offers sudden glimpses and unexpected insights into what was happening to Oxford as a whole, during the period when I was an undergraduate there. The poetry we wrote reflects the attitudes current among those who were reading arts subjects. What one seems to detect in this poetry, looking back, is not merely a reaction against modernism and cosmopolitanism, but an actual contraction of cultural resources.

Whatever class we came from, we had arrived at Oxford as a result of an intensely competitive process, stretching back, for most of us, into the years of early adolescence. Though education had been thrown open to the intellectually gifted—and this, in the fullest sense, was something which had only come about since the war—the education system itself was unchanged in most particulars. It remained what it had been, twenty or even forty years before. This meant, for those whose interests were directed towards the arts, that they had to master the language and concepts of an élite to which they did not necessarily belong by right of birth—as, for example, the denizens of Bloomsbury had belonged to it. Inevitably, they altered what they absorbed.

Since my generation had less 'background' (Bloomsbury's word), we tended, I now think, to make culture narrower. Interdisciplinary researches struck us as untidy. We were insular, less interested in what was going on abroad than our predecessors had been; and we were often, in any case, excluded from foreign experiments by a simple lack of languages. We were far more insistent than pre-war intellectuals had been on precise statements of intention, precise definitions of quality. Where the old élite had tended to be snobbish and hedonistic, the new meritocracy to which we were recruited had a curiously innocent puritanism: art for art's sake was again challenged by the nineteenth-century —and, it must be added, traditionally British—concept of art for morality's sake.

At any rate, my judgement is that the constrictions we imposed on ourselves as beginning writers can still be sensed today, not merely in the poetry produced in England, but in English post-war literature as a whole.

Meanwhile, the number of undergraduate poets enthusiastically at work in the Oxford of the fifties enabled the university Poetry Society to attract distinguished speakers, and for the most part to provide them with large audiences. Humanly, but perhaps paradoxically, we liked the swaggering romantics best as public performers. The biggest crowd, and the greatest success, went inevitably to Dylan Thomas, who was lured into doing a reading in the marvellously inappropriate surroundings of Rhodes House.

Thomas seemed indifferent, not only to the setting—all blond wood and the odour of a decayed imperialism—but to his huge audience, which packed the large hall and the gallery above it. His performance was almost purely narcissistic—self-celebrating, self-massaging. Even when he turned from his own poems to read D. H. Lawrence's 'The Ship of Death', he somehow contrived to make one feel that Lawrence had stolen a march on him, and had slyly managed to write a poem which Thomas himself would have penned, if some unfortunate accident had not released it at a slightly earlier point in the time-scale than had originally been planned.

It became obvious, as the recital proceeded, that the legendary Dylan was a little drunk—indeed, we should have been disappointed if he had not been so. Alcohol had long been part of the legend—long before the publication of posthumous memoirs such as *Dylan Thomas in America*. Perspiration flowed from the bardic brow in great drops, and occasionally the voice stumbled over a phrase, or the tubby body swayed alarmingly. But no disaster occurred, the performance was brought to a triumphant conclusion. One of the organizers described to me afterwards what a sweat of anxiety he and his colleague had been in, not merely to ensure that the star of the evening arrived in Oxford at all, but to top him up to precisely the right degree of tipsiness, but no further. The success of the evening was the proof of the skill with which these delicate operations had been managed. It was no surprise, later, when the master-diplomat in charge became principal poetry editor for the BBC.

A poet who had a less resounding success, but whose visit sticks in the mind, was George Barker. He left us impressed, frightened and puzzled. His refusal to recognize hierarchical decencies, or the merits of reason and order, and his failure to be impressed by the university itself, all upset us. We failed to recognize in him both a survivor from the old pre-war Bohemia, and a precursor, in attitudes if not in speech and dress, of the flower-power hippies who were later to show such a contempt for our own generation of, as they thought, smug conformists. I cannot remember anything that Barker said to us, either at the reading itself or at the various pubs to which we took him afterwards, but I can still recall the amused, ironic glances he darted at us from time to time from under the heavy lids of his eyes.

Not all our visitors were as well received or as flatteringly treated. The irritant occasions were those on which the visiting poet seemed to offer himself for judgement, for execution almost. He appeared before us in the rôle of victim, a rôle not imposed by us but chosen by himself. On the other hand, we seldom or never refused him his wish to suffer at our hands. His readings were received in freezing silence. Any jocular comments he might attempt to make about the poems he had chosen aroused the most superior smiles, and for the most part no smile at all. If there was laughter, it was unsympathetic. These were merely, however, the preliminaries of the bullfight, the skirmishing of the picadors, the placing of the barbs in the bull's neck in order to weaken it. The serious business of the evening came later, at question-time, as the visitor was teased and tormented with barely concealed insolence, until at last someone was ready to run the sword in, right between the shoulder-blades. 'Then why, Mr X, do you write poetry at all?'

In those days, I sometimes wondered at the masochistic impulse which led such poets to visit us. Later, when I began to receive such invitations myself from undergraduate poetry societies, but especially when these came from either Oxford or Cambridge, I began to understand. My first, terrified impulse was always to refuse. But when the time came to write the letter, I found myself sending an acceptance. The fascination which drew me back was the knowledge that here, if anywhere, were to be found rivals I did not as yet know about—competitors for the few and tattered laurel crowns which are all a poet gets for his pains in a modern society. It was worth enduring humiliation to sniff these new contenders out at first hand, to estimate their strengths and weaknesses. Then, too, there was the impulse which I think all poets feel to discover if you are still 'the youngest one' (the phrase is Stravinsky's: 'All my life I have been the youngest one')—for it is a characteristic of poets to insist on youth even after it has long departed. How far would my thoughts and feelings correspond with those of writers who were genuinely much younger than I?

As these painful visits were repeated, at irregular intervals, I began to see, too, that the ordeal was not always the same ordeal, nor indeed was it inevitable. The swift growth and equally swift decay of undergraduate generations meant that the whole climate could change between one sally and the next. If one had been roughly greeted last time, one might just as easily be received with acclamation on a return visit.

CHAPTER SIXTEEN

FINALLY, THERE WERE Oxford friendships which cannot be as rigidly categorized as those which I have already described. Can I, for example, speak of the party-goers as a group? If so, it was a group so large, and so amorphous, that it necessarily included people drawn from all the circles I have described already. Cut adrift from their rôles, the poets and the politicians changed their character, and became just faces in the sea of faces which flowed at random into one set of college rooms or another, night after night.

When I describe these enormous parties to people who came up to Oxford only a short time after I myself departed from it, they are incredulous, and declare that no such social scene existed in their own day—and that surely things must have been more modest, less overblown and impetuous than I remember them to have been? But this was not the case. Anyone who bothers to look up the back issues of *Isis* which cover those years will immediately discover that a self-consciously bitchy gossip-column occupied the most prominent place in the magazine, week after week. This gossip-column was always said to be the feature which chiefly maintained the periodical's circulation, and it did not disappear until the abrupt change of social and political climate in the university during the middle fifties.

It was sometimes difficult to decide if the gossip-column was nourished by the parties, or if the parties were given for the sake of the gossip-column. It was, in any case, the epoch when similar columns in the London dailies were aspiring to new heights of sycophancy and slander; the time of the Dockers, of eloping heiresses, of the Chelsea Set. In this, as in other things, Oxford was determined to ape the metropolis.

But the Oxford party world did, after all, differ from the one to be found in London. Though there were a number of rich undergraduates, it was no good pretending that even the most ambitious undergraduate hosts could rival the resources of the milieu that the *Tatler* and William Hickey described from their respective standpoints. It was seldom, if ever, that one was offered champagne, and seldom enough whisky. The usual drink was sherry, and if one drank too much of it one woke the next morning with the feeling that a man in hobnailed boots had been trampling across one's kidneys. Nor were the guests exceptionally gorgeous in their plumage. The tweed skirt and the check sports-jacket still ruled; the time of cheap fantasy clothes for the young had yet to come.

True, the most fashionable undergraduates—almost exclusively male—had certain affectations. Trousers were worn very tight, not merely at the rump but all the way down, and those most in vogue were made of cavalry twill, rather than of grey flannel. Shoes were suede. Suede desert-boots were particularly smart, and were self-consciously referred to as 'nigger-kickers'. Sports-coats were cut with narrow lapels, tight waists, full skirts, cuffs to the sleeves and exaggeratedly deep single vents. The shape, now I think of it, was rather like that of the silk coats worn by the beaux of the mid-eighteenth century.

To be in the very height of fashion, one had to wear a flowery silk waistcoat, preferably made of the shiniest, gaudiest Chinese silk. These waistcoats gleamed incongruously under the drab tweed of our sportscoats. Strangely, it was less the thing to wear them with a suit. Often, they were worn with a matching tie made of the same material. Alternatively, and in the absence of a waistcoat, it was the thing to wear a tie made of heavy corduroy, tied in a great lumpy knot under one's collar. Other ties were made from equally unsuitable materials, ranging from gold lamé to real snakeskin. Undergraduate actors—but not the rest of us unless we were going punting—wore open-necked shirts, and filled in the neck with a cravat, a fashion modelled on thirties photographs of London matinée idols.

After the night's party there was the ritual of going out to dinner at certain restaurants. The point about these restaurants was not that they cooked well, but that they were said to 'have atmosphere'. The walls were always covered in heavy red-flock wallpaper, and there were numerous gilded mirrors and gilt sconces. Candles stuck in champagne bottles stood on the tables; the lighting, apart from the glare from these, was minimal. What we ate, and, mercifully, we were often too drunk to taste it, was flabby pâté, unripe avocados, and stringy slices of meat drowned in acrid sauces, with frozen vegetables to accompany them. Ratatouille was a staple offering: a ratatouille Provence would have disowned, at once insipid and faintly rancid.

Some of these restaurants were in Oxford itself and some were outside, in Woodstock or Abingdon or even as far away as Henley. The ones outside Oxford were perhaps considered the smarter, because getting to them meant that one of the party had to own a car. Car-ownership was the ultimate status-symbol. It is surprising that the wild drunken drives along dark Oxfordshire roads that these expeditions entailed did not lead to a series of fatal crashes, or, at the least, to arrests and rustications.

As a non car-owner, I was commonly confined to patronizing the smart restaurants of Oxford itself. My then favourite, and the most expensive of them, was a smallish room on the first floor of a house in the High, which you entered via the bar on ground level. At this bar there mingled uneasily the noisier and more exhibitionist part of undergraduate society, and servicemen from the American bases that then surrounded Oxford. It was strange how the two groups contrived never to coalesce. The room looked as if one photographic transparency had been superimposed upon another, taken in the same place, but on a totally different occasion.

Upstairs was undergraduate territory. The servicemen seldom ventured there. One saw, however, a few outsiders: dons currying favour with their pupils, for purposes either social or sexual; and a few ambiguous people who existed in the university without being of it, the men older by ten years than most of those present, but wearing a more opulent and fanciful version of current undergraduate modes, and the girls (only one or two of these) both more confidently beautiful and infinitely more soignée than their undergraduate sisters. The best-looking of them all was the hardest to place, either socially or indeed financially. Some years later she surfaced in the popular press, having acquired a Balkan title and involved in some minor social mishap.

Another of the group, male, and famous for the extravagance of his entertainments, took somewhat longer to contrive a reappearance in my life. I was attending a private view, at a time when this book was already begun, when Marty drifted through the gallery door, and greeted me as if he had come on purpose to find me. At a first glance, his appearance was little changed: his face was as florid as ever, his gestures had the same expansiveness, his hair still rose over a broad but conspicuously wrinkled forehead in a silver quiff. It was only after a moment's scrutiny that one recognized the differences. The fingernails of the plump hands were long and filthy, the fine ring gone—it had been replaced by something tawdry which might have been won at a fairground—and the fat jowl was unshaven and dewed with a fine sweat. Marty had always liked velvet suits, but the one he now wore was covered with stains and droppings, and looked as if he had slept in it. The collar of his cream silk shirt—another foible I remember from the past—was threadbare as well as grimy. As he came closer, and took my hand, there came from him a graveyard odour. It was soon clear that he was desperately in need of money, and that a bed for the night would also be welcome. Despite the food of his I had eaten in the past, and the numerous drinks swallowed in the past—Pimm's No. 1 was a favourite tipple—this apparition dismayed me. Poor Marty now seemed the living allegory of the tawdriness of all those undergraduate nights, conjured up because I had begun to think of them again.

The special character of those Oxford nights can, however, be more exactly given, not by describing Marty and his like, but by speaking of the position of women. In theory, at least, the university was now a bisexual institution, but this was a fact one would never have guessed from many of the parties that I attended. It was not that these entertainments were overtly homosexual, but it was clear that the young males who formed the majority of the guests were embarrassed by and even terrified of the few girls. The only women who succeeded in making their presence felt were those who consented to be 'characters'.

The future Balkan aristocrat, for all her good looks, only kept her social footing by descending to this—we were fascinated, not by her beauty, but by her raucous Glasgow accent, which won her many invitations.

The queen bee of Oxford parties was neither young nor beautiful. Enid Starkie appeared at many of them in her scarlet jacket and trousers, a glass in her hand, a little beret clapped rakishy sideways on her greying curls. Everywhere she went an adoring court of undergraduates surrounded her. In part, this was due to simple snobbery—Enid was then approaching the height of her celebrity as an expert on French literature, both within the university and outside it. But partly, as I sensed, she put us at our ease because she was a woman with no hint of sexual threat or sexual mystery, at least to us twenty-one-year-olds.

When a girl who did not understand the Oxford rules and the Oxford atmosphere swam into our orbit, the effects could be both embarrassing and comic. One undergraduate, a member of the literary set and also of my college, acquired a girl-friend in the course of a Long Vacation visit to America. In due course she came to see him in Oxford. From the start it was clear that the trip was not going to be a success. Sylvia was a member of a rich New York family, very pretty, and always, by our standards, rather too elaborately dressed. She floated along in pastel-coloured silk dresses, skirts belling out over stiffened petticoats. The trouble was that she expected to be the focus of attention everywhere she went. Not only must her official escort hover by her chair, bring her a drink, light her cigarette, fetch her handbag, help her into her coat as soon as she wanted to go, but the rest of us, too, must play our appointed parts in the game of courtly love. Sylvia made it clear, with gestures and glances rather than words, that she noted and disapproved of any lapse in carrying out the ritual. At first, fascinated by her elegance, we allowed ourselves to be blackmailed into doing as she expected. But soon we grew bored with her. Our natural gaucheness reasserted itself. More and more often Sylvia found herself left alone in a corner with the proclaimed object of her affections. With this she was not content. Nor, after a few days, was he. Both he and she soon reached the stage where they would seize any excuse to avoid being left alone together—she, because she found it insulting not to have a more numerous escort; he, because, now a prey to insecurity, she worked him twice as hard.

If the refinements of courtship were beyond many of us, so, too, was sex in its blunter and coarser aspects. Sometimes, when the evening's party at last began to die—for I would seldom rouse myself and leave early—I would make my way, not to the restaurant of the moment, but to the cheap cafés at the beginning of the Cowley Road, which stayed open till the small hours for the sake of American service personnel, and for the sad whores who made their living from the soldiers. One especially dingy café was my favourite, and one ugly prostitute with a wall-eye particularly fascinated me. I would sit alone, or with a friend whom I had dragged there to keep me company, slowly sipping a cup of bad coffee, listening to the juke-box, and glancing at her covertly. She never seemed to notice this scrutiny, but went on laughing and joking with her pick-up of the night. Not once did we speak to one another.

Fortunately, there were girls in Oxford more amusing than either American princesses or local prostitutes. The male students might not always understand how to approach their female contemporaries, but the latter, though much less numerous, were more sophisticated and more relaxed than the boys who were often so frightened of them. Somehow—it is perhaps significant that I cannot recall the exact mechanism—I became friendly with a group of girls from St Anne's, who lived in a large house called Cherwell Edge. Visiting a friend there was, even in those days, an event surrounded with strange ceremonies and conventions. One could not just walk in. One had to be announced, fetched from the front hall, and then one's hostess would walk in front of one, self-consciously shouting the word 'Man!' as one passed through the corridors, in order to warn any of the other occupants who might be in a state of undress. Understandably, few of the girls could manage to do this with a straight face, and one's progress would be punctuated with outbursts of giggles.

I soon fell in love with one of the inhabitants of Cherwell Edge, but it was an unsatisfactory affair for both of us. The chief reason was my constitutional timidity. Marguerite was a slim, cat-like girl—she hated the adjective 'boyish' and would indignantly push her breasts forward under her tight sweater if one used it, and demand a retraction. Her resemblance to a cat was accentuated by the fact that she was extremely short-sighted, and wore tip-tilted spectacles of a kind more fashionable then than they are now.

What attracted me to her was her aggressive independence. She thought many aspects of Oxford life were nonsensical, and said so, usually with the hope that she would be overheard by someone in authority. She only had to be told that something was forbidden to be seized with a desire to attempt it. For example, she insisted on being punted through the stretch of the Cherwell called Parson's Pleasure—the waters of this nude bathing place, as well as the banks, were strictly forbidden to women. She was immensely amused by the flash of naked buttocks, as the bathers sprang for cover, in the river or elsewhere.

Surprisingly enough, Marguerite was a virgin. She regarded this condition as both shameful and burdensome, and was determined to remedy the situation during her time at university. If she ever considered me as the means of doing so, she soon discarded the idea. I was her constant escort, her *cavaliere servente*, but these were more serious matters. She formed a plan and carried it out with characteristic ruthlessness. Of course she went too far.

The first I heard of Marguerite's downfall was when she summoned me to have tea with her in one of the cafés in the Cornmarket. Tea and scones were no sooner ordered than she informed me that she was being sent down by her college. In fact, she was, at that moment, not supposed to be in Oxford at all. She had not even been allowed the time to pack her trunk: the other girls at Cherwell Edge could do it for her, and it would then be sent on. The reason was that she had been out of the building all night, and (I can still hear the exclamation mark in her voice) 'with a man!' The fact that the college authorities had so rapidly discovered what she was up to was less a tribute to their acumen than to Marguerite's spirit of defiance. She had been careful to leave them all the clues they could possibly have needed.

Of course, Marguerite took every opportunity she could to appear in Oxford thereafter, simply because she was forbidden to be there. Nevertheless, our relationship languished, though I also continued to see her from time to time in the vacations. Before we drifted apart, we had a strange mutual encounter with her lover of that first night. We were walking towards the Martyrs' Memorial when he passed us on the same pavement, but going in the opposite direction. 'That's him,' said Marguerite. 'You know, the man I got sent down for.' 'Why didn't you say hello to him?' I asked, perhaps naïvely. Marguerite paused, thought for a moment, licked her lips, and then said conclusively: 'Because he's got a face like an unwashed plate.' We never referred to the subject again.

By the time my last year at Oxford came, I had achieved celebrity of a sort—but not as an actor, politician or poet, and certainly not as an amorist. I had become famous for going to parties. I was a talisman of a sort, and it was mandatory to invite me. The more parties I went to, the more depressed I got. Arriving at the beginning of the evening, I would rouse myself, talk animatedly, make the jokes and tell the stories that were now expected of me—for I had, at least, learnt to sing for my supper. Then, as the room filled up, I would gradually move away from the centre. I often spent the last half of the party by myself in a corner, sitting on a window-seat perhaps, half-hidden by a curtain, talking to those who came up to me, but deliberately letting the talk lapse into longer and longer silences, until they were driven away.

These depressions, bad enough at Oxford, deepened during the vacations. I found it impossible to get on with my vacation reading, but sat idly for hours, a text-book open on my lap, unable even to bring myself to turn the pages. One escape was to creep off to the various cartoon cinemas in the Charing Cross Road, where I would watch, but with scarcely a titter, the frenetic adventures of Donald Duck and Mr Magoo. I frequently saw the same programme round twice or even three times.

Another escape was to go to the swimming-pool at Dolphin Square. In the afternoons this was often entirely deserted, and I would swim up and down, doing lengths, until I was exhausted.

Occasionally, however, there were other visitors. The most frequent, in addition to myself, were Diana Dors, then no more than a starlet, her hair dyed flaming red rather than platinum blonde, together with her first husband, Dennis Gittings, and the two rival 'Winslow Boys'—Anthony Newley, who had had the part in the West End run of the play, and Neil North, who had been given the rôle when the play was filmed. Neil North and I had been at school together, and knew one another, so I was allowed, though not positively encouraged, to join the gang.

Dors never swam. She knelt on the edge of the pool in a green satin bathing-suit, much boned around the bosom (it made her look like a melting ice-cream cone) and placidly watched the antics of the others, as they chased one another, or fell into the pool with squeaky cries of alarm. Newley and North looked a bit like Donald Duck and Mr Magoo.

Strangely enough, the approach of Final Examinations played no part in lowering my spirits, though I knew that, in the course of the last year, I had not been doing nearly enough work. I revised in moderation, but there were no frantic all-night sessions in preparation for the ordeal. My fellow historians at Merton began to look pale and worn; I continued on my accustomed course. My relations with my tutors were in what was now their usual condition, that of armed truce.

When the day of the first paper arrived, my mood of confidence persisted. I sat down, answered the necessary number of questions at what looked to me like the right length, glanced over what I had written, and left the examination room with half an hour to go.

Each succeeding paper went more or less the same way. I was, of course, aware that I had dealt with some better than I had with others. And I was under no illusions that I was doing well enough to get or deserve the first that others had once promised me, and which I had even gone so far as to promise to myself. I knew that I was not cutting down through the surface of the subjects I was required to write about, giving proof that I had grasped and understood them. I was, indeed, rather struck by the competent superficiality of my answers when I read them through before I handed them in, and also by their innate dreariness. I felt a kind of sadness, at long last, about an opportunity missed: an opportunity to make something of all the information I had obediently but reluctantly absorbed, something which had the breath of life in it. I did not know whether to blame my tutors, my text-books or myself. Perhaps humanly, I felt the blame could not be all mine. But I also felt a profound relief that this was the last hurdle in the educational steeplechase. I was tired of going over the jumps at other people's behest. It was nearly time to discover my own challenges.

CHAPTER SEVENTEEN

WHEN I CAME down from Oxford there followed a period of hanging about. I was waiting for two things: my Oxford viva, and my call-up papers.

The viva was, as I had expected, a formality. At the end of the brief interview, I was given the verdict: 'A good Second, but never considered for a First.' I had, in fact, done slightly better than either my tutors or I expected. Yet, strangely, this brief sentence was like a door slamming. Despite everything, I had, when I thought about the future, thought of myself in a university context. It seemed impossible that I should leave the safe world of scholarship entirely. But universities, on the whole, do not offer fellowships to the owners of good second-class degrees.

As far as National Service went, I felt a little more confident about it than I had done as a schoolboy, but not much. I had at any rate passed a selection board for a commission in the RAF Education Service, and knew that I would be posted almost straight to Officer Cadet Training Unit. Getting through this board had, I think, been a close-run thing: it was clear that the officers responsible for selection found me an odd fish. One persistently asked me 'if I thought I could lead men'. Stubbornly I replied that I had so far met few situations in which I had failed to get my own way. It was true, but it can hardly have been endearing.

The call to the colours was slow in coming. I passed an aimless few weeks. For the first time since early childhood, I had nothing in view, no objective. But at last a letter arrived, curtly ordering me to report to RAF Cardington in Bedfordshire. After a few days there I would go on to OCTU.

At Cardington, I had my first stroke of luck. In charge of my hut was a Jamaican corporal. Even though I was white, I was the only Jamaican he had yet encountered among all the recruits entrusted to him. As a tribute to this fact, he insisted on sewing on for me all the numerous name tags and badges with which we had been issued. Meanwhile my companions—all of them destined for the RAF ground officers' OCTU like myself—struggled with unfamiliar needles and thread. They also struggled with newly issued black boots, passing round tips gleaned from older brothers, or from school-friends who had already served their time. Spoons were heated over matches, and the hut soon had a fine stink of warm boot-polish. Boots had immediately become one of the main topics of conversation among the members of our squad. Only I was debarred from offering an opinion.

In a determined effort to avoid having to look after these fetish objects (I knew they would get me into trouble), I had already persuaded the camp doctor that boots were something I was medically unfit to wear. This exemption was to single me out, not always favourably, for the rest of my service career.

The other main topic at Cardington was how to get leave. Newly inducted conscripts were told that everything off camp was also off limits. Weekend passes were quite out of the question. As potential officers, we took this as an affront to our as yet un-tested sense of responsibility.

Particularly affronted was the man who had the bed next to mine. Splendidly blond, typically public school in accent and bearing, he gave, within twenty-four hours of our arrival, every sign of being an accomplished skyver in the true service tradition. His bed-space never got swept; his kit was never ready for in-spection. It fell to me, and to his other next-door neighbour, to remedy his deficiencies in these respects—the team-spirit of the hut already demanded it. Yet Stephenson (as I shall call him) never attracted blame for this because he obviously felt no guilt. His lazy charm conquered all. It even conquered the commanding officer at Cardington, who was persuaded to issue Stephenson with the only weekend pass that any member of our squad re-ceived. So far as we could discover, it was the only pass issued to any of the new intake of conscripts. When the weekend came, the rest of us mooned aimlessly about, looking for something to do.

The RAF, wiser in these matters than we had taken it to be,

came up with at least one answer to the problem. A disused hangar had been converted into a vast dance-hall; bus-loads of local factory and shop girls were shipped in every Saturday night. It must have been strange for them, arriving week after week to find a complete change of partners. But much practice apparently made perfect—I soon discovered that all the girls were formidably good performers, with a fierce intolerance of those, such as myself, who were not as skilled as they were. After a few sweating embarrassed turns round the immense floor, which was bathed in a dim red light, I lost my courage and slipped away to the barrack hut and a paperback.

The day soon came when we were to be shipped out of this limbo. We crammed our kit into our kit-bags, and were in turn crammed into a train for London. A change of stations; a long dismal wait, and we found ourselves on the train for Liverpool, en route for Jurby, on the northernmost tip of the Isle of Man. The journey was broken by a night's stay in a squalid barracks at Birkenhead—it was our first glimpse of the soft underbelly of service life, with its peeling paint, dirty beds, stinking toilets and shortage of cutlery. Most of us had not yet washed and polished our mess-tins. Dinner tasted slightly of sewing-machine oil.

Next morning we boarded the ferry for Douglas, then took the toy train which linked the two ends of the island. Any hopes we might have entertained were immediately dashed by the sight of Jurby itself. The camp was bleak, fit for its function as a kind of purgatory. Its low huts were built of asbestos, and they were arranged in regular lines under an enormous sky. As we arrived, the sun was just setting, and the whole of this sky was filled with tones of mother-of-pearl, salmon-pink and silver. The characterless low buildings and concrete paths dwindled to insignificance beneath this display.

Tension filled our lives at OCTU. We knew we were always under observation; always on trial. Every action, however trivial, counted for something in the dossier that was being built up. In addition, we were always tired. The training involved a tremendous amount of physical exertion.

Everything at Jurby was organized by 'courses'. Within the camp at any one time there were always three of these, at various stages of their training. The courses in turn, were divided according to the huts which their members happened to inhabit. In theory, course-loyalty took second place only to hut-loyalty. You hung together or were liable to be hanged separately.

It soon became obvious, however, that our course would not be a good one—at least as the authorities defined it. Few of the ingredients of group loyalty were present. We fell into three different and opposing categories. First, there were the senior NCOs, qualifying for commissions at the end of their service careers. They would never get beyond Flight Lieutenant, but it meant a better pension. The members of this category were old sweats to a man—wise in the ways of the service, hard-drinking, cunning and (in their own estimation) tough. But, whatever else it had taught them, the service had not encouraged them to think for themselves.

Then there were the cadets who had signed up for short-service commissions—three years instead of two. Most were on the rebound from something, either a failed examination or a failed love-affair. In comparison to the members of the third category, ourselves, the National Service cadets, the short-service men enjoyed a privileged position, not only in their own eyes, but in those of the authorities. Their skills were those which the RAF thought it needed—most of them were accountants. And they had committed themselves for long enough for these skills to be of some use. In return, they were not only paid better than the National Servicemen, but (as it later appeared) there were heavy pressures on the camp commandant to pass them as fit for command. We alone could expect no mercy.

The OCTU had a deliberately exhausting routine. What free moments we had were passed either in studying air-force regulations, or in cleaning our kit. We robbed ourselves of sleep in order to maintain the standard of smartness required of us. There was no official lights-out, and the lights burned very late in our huts. This lack of sleep and lack of regulation soon caused tension in the barrack-room which I inhabited. One of our number, a National Serviceman like myself, was a man whom I shall call Mooney. He was plump, pale, slow, disorganized and obsessional. The lights blazed until well past midnight as he sat cross-legged on his bed, clumsily blancoing and reblancoing his webbing, or polishing and repolishing his boots. Reveille was at five in the morning, and tempers rapidly grew frayed.

As it happened, I alone had some reason to be grateful to Mooney. He was to some extent my companion in misfortune. He and I were undoubtedly the two least military-looking cadets in the camp. RAF battledress did not become either of us—we looked like two sacks of potatoes tied in the middle. On the barrack-square, when ordered to slope arms, we tended to wrap our rifles round our necks, as if they were lengths of limp spaghetti. We marched, so the two of us were told, like a couple of pregnant ducks.

Mooney always had particular trouble with his uniform. Any pair of trousers he put on immediately fell out of crease. His battledress jacket looked as if he kept it wadded up in a ball at the bottom of his locker. My sartorial difficulty was perhaps less serious, since it led to ridicule rather than to black marks. The first time that the drill sergeant addressed me, it was on the subject of my beret. 'Change it at stores!' he yelled. 'The one you've got on looks like a pimple on a pumpkin.' I duly changed it for a larger size, but however much I twisted this, wadded it or folded it, it continued to look absurd.

I also, as it turned out, had a slight advantage over Mooney in two other ways. The more obvious of these became apparent when we were detailed, as every cadet was in turn, to drill a squad of fellow-cadets. Mooney was unable to raise his voice. I, on the other hand, had a loud voice and used it without inhibition. As they marched, wheeled, changed step, came to a halt, stood at attention, stood at ease, all to my word of command, the warrant officers and the short-service commissions eyed me with a mixture of resentment and respect.

The other advantage appeared when we were turned loose on the camp assault-course. Of all the rumoured horrors of service life, this was the one which had frightened me the most in prospect. As on other occasions in my life, I soon discovered that if one cannot be spectacularly competent, it is sometimes best to be spectacularly incompetent. I frightened myself silly on the nets we were asked to climb, the narrow planks we were expected to traverse. But I frightened the officer in charge of us still more. He was in bad odour for the number of broken limbs his methods produced. He did not want to add me to his score. His nerve cracked slightly before mine did. Unobtrusively, he began shepherding me away from the more dangerous corners of his domain. Poor Mooney, pleased to excel me in this, trundled round after the others, always out of breath and a moment or two behind.

Neither he nor I could avoid attracting the unfavourable attention of those responsible for training us. This tended to make both of us pariahs among our fellow-cadets. No one wanted to be associated with potential failure. This was made plain to me when the time came for our first night exercise. We were arbitrarily split up into small parties of four or five. My party included two of the younger NCOs, who told me bluntly that I would be in all senses a burden on their progress, and must do exactly as I was told.

Our set task was to cross a long stretch of moor and bog high up in the centre of the island, with the help of a flashlight, pocket compass, and map. A bus dropped us at regular intervals along one road, and we were instructed to rendezvous at a pub on another road which ran parallel to the first, but some miles distant.

As we got off the vehicle, my arms were grabbed by my two burly companions. 'Come on,' they said. 'We're going to do it this way.' Thus linked, we set off across country at a brisk gallop, ignoring easier gradients and possible detours. Once we encountered a small stream. My companions jumped; I stumbled, and fell about six feet down the steps of a small waterfall which had been hidden by the darkness and the bracken. Drenched but uninjured, I scrambled out, and our headlong progress was resumed. As it happened, this ducking in mountain water made little difference, as the ragged clouds which had from time to time hidden the moon now thickened, and a downpour started. Everyone was soon as wet as I was. It didn't seem to matter. I shook off the hands which still clutched me under the elbows, and began to run, more easily and freely than I would have thought possible. We found a small cart-track which we had already marked on the map as leading almost directly to the point of rendezvous. It sloped downhill, and we pelted along it, jumping from tussock to tussock on the middle ridge. The moon reappeared, and shone in the water which brimmed in the ruts on either side.

At the pub, we were the second party to arrive. Seeing me, our predecessors greeted us with something like incredulity. It took the edge off their success when one of the course duds turned up hard on their heels. Our speed did us little practical good, however. The camp transportation arrangements had broken down, and we spent hours shivering by the roadside, even after the last stragglers had arrived, waiting to be picked up.

Warned by this experience, I resolved to tackle our next exercise—'escape and evasion'—in a more practical spirit. We were to be dropped individually at various points some distance from camp. Our task was to make our way back into the camp itself without being spotted and captured. I already knew, from camp gossip, that few cadets succeeded in this. The pursuers were well acquainted with the chosen stretch of countryside; we knew it, of course, not at all. Basically there were two choices. The first, and most logical if one meant to succeed, was to stay off the roads—to skulk from farmyard to farmyard and hilltop to hilltop, until at last one got near enough to the objective to make a dash for it. The obvious points of danger were any roads which one might have to cross; and the flat, bare land which surrounded the camp itself. On the other hand, there was another choice, preferable if one thought success to be not only improbable but unnecessary. This was to make what progress one could on the road itself, thus pursuing one's pursuers.

Equipped with a packed lunch and a paperback, I waited tranquilly for some hours in a small wood, until I thought the first captures must already have been made—a distant droning of motor-engines told me that activity was taking place somewhere in the neighbourhood. I then walked down to the nearest road and began to plod in the direction of Jurby. For an hour or so, nobody appeared; I began to wonder if insolence might not carry me through, at the price of a long and tedious walk. But suddenly, blessedly, there was a shout. I made the ritual attempt to escape, but was soon seized, and was bundled into a bus, already occupied, I was happy to note, by seven or eight other cadets.

We motored through the Manx lanes, and more and more captives were shoved through the door. Once again, I pulled out my paperback. As it happened, nobody succeeded in getting through, though two cadets were caught only as they approached the camp perimeter. I had not made myself fatally conspicuous.

One day, in the middle of the course, I was summoned to the camp commandant's office, handed a rail warrant, and told to report to a medical board in London. My hearing, it seemed, must immediately be re-tested. Something in the medical record was causing concern.

I rattled down from Jurby in the toy train, and boarded the ferry. The weather was threatening and I had provided myself with seasickness tablets from the camp dispensary. Two were to be taken an hour before sailing, so I swallowed them immediately I got on board. Almost at once an announcement was made over the ship's tannoy. Because of adverse weather conditions, departure would be delayed. Similar announcements were made at intervals for the next twelve hours. Gradually I consumed my whole supply of tablets, becoming aware, as I did so, of a strange buzzing in my head.

I recall very little of the voyage or of the train journey to London, and equally little of the medical examination, for which I arrived in the nick of time. Glancing at myself in a mirror in the hall of the building, I noticed that my pupils were much dilated. The buzzing was still with me, like a distant hive. I explained the circumstances to the ear-nose-and-throat specialist, who grimaced and scribbled something at random on his pad. I was still, in his opinion, fit for service.

In the afternoon, before catching the return train to Liverpool, I was free to visit Richard Buckle's Diaghilev exhibition, then on at Forbes House near Hyde Park Corner. My head buzzing louder than ever, I wandered through the successive rooms within which Buckle had created the first of the 'multi-media environments'—though the term itself had not yet been invented. Wafts of *Mitsuko* (Diaghilev's favourite scent) and the strains of Stravinsky ballet music crept up upon the visitor at every turn. The exhibition was hot, luxurious, secretive, magical, claustrophobic and almost deserted. I could hardly believe that Jurby and Forbes House existed on the same planet.

Back on the Isle of Man I found that, though my medical status had been settled, my future as an officer was still very much in question. The climax of the course, an ordeal much whispered about, was a week's camp on the shores of the Irish Sea, at a spot yet bleaker than the one occupied by Jurby itself. This camp would be entirely officered and run by the cadets; our instructors would be there as observers only. I had been selected as camp commandant for one of the six days (posts changed in rotation every day), and as chief warrant officer for another day later in the week. To be thus singled out was no compliment, as honours of this kind were usually given to those most likely to founder beneath them.

My mood, therefore, was not particularly cheerful as we marched towards the appointed spot. Our rifles were carried slung on the shoulder—a simple knack I had never mastered. Every few hundred yards the sling dropped jarringly and I was forced to hitch it up again. The camp-site, when we reached it, was as unprepossessing as we had been promised—a stretch of sand-dune, covered with scrubby grass and a few thorn-bushes, and pocked with innumerable rabbit holes. The rabbits themselves were absent, for this was the period when myxomatosis raged. Occasionally one found a pathetic heap of bones at the entrance to one of the burrows.

We fell out of ranks and began to set up camp. The results were predictably chaotic. We knew very little about tents, tarpaulins, field-kitchens and the rest. As I watched the panicky efforts of my companions I began to revise, not so much my estimate of them, as their estimate of me. My turn as commanding officer began at dawn the next morning, and I promised myself that things would go differently.

They were indeed different. I shouted. I raged. I bullied. I ran up and down. By the end of the day we were organized. I had knocked down one image of myself and created another.

The days passed; I found to my surprise that my spirits had risen and continued to rise. Everyone else's seemed to sink in about the same measure. The inhabitants of the camp became increasingly dishevelled, bad tempered and exhausted. Nevertheless what seemed to come back to me, at this incongruous moment, was the pleasure of childhood picnics, open-air eating and sleeping, barbecues and bonfires. The weather was warm for late autumn; sea and sky alike were mantled in a gentle haze. At night, there were exercises, conducted with hilarious incompetence by cadets and instructors alike.

The fifth day came and it was my turn to be chief NCO. Mooney was to be commanding officer. We were packing up, ready for next morning's departure. Already conscious that I had escaped the axe, I determined to rescue Mooney if I could. My plan was simple. The instructors lived in a wooden tower, once a coastal signalling station, at one end of the camp, which straggled away northward under the lee of a dune. There was plenty to be done. I would therefore organize matters near the tower and cookhouse; Mooney would busy himself in the distance where minor errors and muddles would, with any luck, remain undetected. I reckoned without Mooney himself. Every five minutes or so he would come drifting up to me, like the matchstick in a bucket which inevitably seeks out the other matchstick floating there. I was aware that these constant consultations—and the reasons for them—were being noted. But even when I managed to drag Mooney out of earshot of official eavesdroppers my warnings had no effect.

It was a sad little band that shambled towards Jurby and our comfortable centrally-heated huts. In many cases the façade of military toughness had been badly fissured. I tended to get some of the blame for this—perhaps I now wore a slight air of self-satisfaction. But in any case there was no longer any need to keep up the pretence of mutual liking. The course was at an end; the results were posted. An unusually high number had failed, or were to be 're-coursed'. The camp commandant was overheard shouting down the telephone to London, arguing with some personage at the Air Ministry, who was issuing instructions that the short-service accountants must be saved at all costs.

CHAPTER EIGHTEEN

As ONE OF those who had passed at OCTU, my next posting, with the rest of the education officers, was to the RAF Education School near Grantham in Lincolnshire. This would be a kind of holiday after our ordeals at Jurby, or so everyone assured us.

The Education School, when we reached it, was a guest-unit at a station largely concerned with other things. With our stripes newly on our shoulders, we were quickly made aware that we counted not merely as second-rate but as fourth-rate citizens. This applied particularly to our position in the mess—a gaunt red-brick building with freezing cold bedrooms, inadequately warmed by coal fires for which there was never enough coal (we were now in the depths of an East Anglian winter). Unable to use our rooms during the day, we also found that a great many other parts of the building were barred to us at most times, including the only comfortable bar and the television room. In a draughty ante-room specially assigned to us, another television set blared, making it impossible either to read or to talk. It was not a cheap mess, and fixed charges made heavy inroads into the salary of a National Service pilot officer. We felt that our miserable pay was being used to subsidize the comforts of others, and the atmosphere was soon one of discontent.

The commandant of the school reacted to our complaints with governessy prissiness. It was clear that his main anxiety was to avoid offending the officers from other branches of the service who shared the mess with us. He soon singled me out as a threat to the precarious harmony he maintained with the rest of the station, and nagged me with especial persistence. My classroom experiences were also discouraging. The airmen and airwomen whom we were set to teach had served as guinea-pigs to so many young educationists that they eyed us with hostile cynicism.

Luckily, the course lasted only a month. At the end of that

time our real service careers were to begin. I found that I had been assigned to Upavon, the headquarters of RAF Transport Command, to serve as junior education officer in the small unit that did the necessary housekeeping and donkey-work.

It was not, at first sight, a plum job. Upavon went back to the days of the Royal Flying Corps. It lay in the middle of Salisbury Plain, and it was thirteen miles from the nearest railway station, from which, in any case, as the timetable showed, the trains ran very infrequently.

When I arrived it was to find a mess almost as large as the one I had just left. It was filled with a frightening swarm of high-ranking officers—almost nothing lower than a wing commander. But the atmosphere was very different from that which prevailed at Grantham.

My first duty was to report officially to my new commanding officer. He was a thin man of medium height, with a ramrod back, a red face, a toothbrush moustache and startling blue eyes. He glared at me, and I quaked. His opening remarks gave me to understand that he did not think much of the education service or education officers. He then read me my confidential reports —a little ceremony which took place on the occasion of every new posting. That from Jurby was flattering, startlingly so. That from Grantham was quite the opposite. My new CO finished his reading, looked up at me, and, for the first time, smiled. 'Well, we know which of those two to believe, don't we?' he said. It was clear that, from his point of view, the two opposing opinions did not cancel one another out; they were both commendations.

The next thing was to meet my new colleague, the head of the station education section. Peter was a north-countryman, holder of a short-service commission, and only a few years older than I. I liked him at once. Though by nature very easy-going, he was also a congenital enthusiast, ready to be pleased by almost everything life had to offer. He had a light, rapid voice, always in full spate, with characteristic short north-country vowels. I found his accent and manner of speaking infectious, to the point where, after only a few weeks, we were often mistaken for one another on the telephone.

My duties turned out to be more curious than onerous. At that epoch, RAF education officers undertook two different kinds of professional activity. The first was general education. All airmen and airwomen were required to attend classes at the education section for a given number of hours a week. This provision was linked to the acts which enforced conscription itself; it served as a kind of sop to those who felt that military service should be used in order to raise the general quality of life. The educational 'opportunity' was extended not merely to conscripts but to young regulars and members of the WRAF.

Even if one had taken it seriously—which, it must be confessed, Peter and I did not—it would have been hard to make the system of general education work. Since the RAF did not accept illiterates, we did not find ourselves with the burden of remedial teaching which seemed to fill up the time of educational sergeants in the Army. Our job was merely to 'extend horizons'. But how? Our pupils, for the most part, were reluctant. They felt they had finished with the classroom when they left school, and thank God for it. The other section commanders on the station were disinclined to release their airmen and airwomen into our charge at times which always turned out to be inconvenient. We could never count on regular attendances. Every period in the classroom had therefore to be a separate disquisition on some topic that the audience might with luck find interesting, but most probably would not.

In despair, we fell back on poetry readings and music appreciation classes. The latter, in particular, were moderately popular with both teacher and taught, because no effort had to be made on either side. On one occasion I played a whole side of the Tchaikovsky Violin Concerto at 78 instead of 33 r.p.m. A wild screeching filled the room, but nobody commented.

The only kind of general educational activity which had much hope of making an impression on our pupils was the 'educational visit'; but these, since each of them swallowed up an entire afternoon and required the use of station transport, were even harder to organize than our classes. Nevertheless, we undertook a good number. We would take a three-ton truck and set out for some local point of interest: a pork-pie factory at Calne, or the railway works at Swindon, or even Stonehenge. The pork-pie factory was chiefly notable for the neatness and speed with which the women who worked there removed the shells from the hard-boiled eggs which were put at the centre of mass-produced scotch eggs and veal-and-ham pies. They did it one-handed, crushing the shell and stripping it off with a single rolling motion of palm and fingers. The railway works were splendidly old-fashioned, a series of tableaux from the early days of the Industrial Revolution. Stonehenge was Stonehenge. It impressed even our young air-women, the toughest nuts of all in the classroom.

The rest of our teaching work pursued different and more strictly limited aims. We prepared people for promotion examinations within the air force, or we tried to tutor them for examinations outside, sometimes up to university entrance level.

The service examinations were very simple tests of competence in writing English and in simple arithmetic. To a middle-class product of a scholarship-mill, such as myself, these classes were (and I do not think I exaggerate at all) the revelation of another England. I was shattered to discover how poorly most of those who came to me had been taught during their years in the clutches of the state education system. True, they now had quite specific reasons, such as they had not possessed before, for wanting to acquire basic skills with words and figures. But it was also a little frightening, as well as depressing, to discover what inhibitions they had about the learning process, and how much they tended to undervalue their own intelligence. Few of my pupils were genuinely stupid, though most of them wrote an English which was so poor as to be almost unintelligible.

Within a few months, however, I had managed to devise a rough-and-ready, but also effective and rapid, way of teaching all but the most inhibited to express themselves. A topic was chosen; a random list of words and ideas associated with it was compiled, using a process of free association; the contents of these lists were then categorized. By the time this was done, the pupil discovered that his essay, in outline form at least, already lay before him on the paper. When he could no longer protest that he could 'think of nothing to say, sir' it was easier to instil the knack of constructing coherent sentences and paragraphs.

Using this method, it was often possible to achieve a dramatic improvement within the space of two or three sessions. Those I taught were openly grateful to me, as well as being astonished to find that matters went so easily. I was equally grateful to them and equally astonished. I discovered that I was, if only intermittently, getting more satisfaction from RAF life than I had from my time at university.

The pupils we had to prepare for outside examinations, mostly School and Higher Certificate, were a more difficult problem, and sometimes stretched our joint resources uncomfortably. I grappled with a classical Latin I had largely forgotten, and with mathematical methods I had never learned.

Only occasionally did one meet with a difficulty that proved to be insoluble. The strangest of these concerned a strapping young corporal, newly married, who was anxious to celebrate his marital status by getting promotion. In every respect but one he was well qualified. At his service duties he was excellent, by all accounts, and certainly his English showed perhaps the most dramatic improvement that I encountered in any of my pupils. But Corporal Smith had no head for figures. The mere sight of them on the page seemed to throw him into a kind of catatonic state; you would see his big shoulders stiffen while his eyes became fixed and glazed. The twice-times multiplication table was an unhappy guessing game, the three-times table most visibly a nightmare. Try as I would, even to the point of suggesting that he jot seven threes down on the margin of his paper, and add them up to discover the answer to three times seven, I could discover no means of getting numbers to perform the most elementary of their evolutions for Corporal Smith.

Frustrated in his hopes of promotion, he became less of a paragon. The last time I saw him he was in the station guardroom, locked up for taking a bicycle without permission. We sat on the edge of his mattress together, and went through the multiplication tables once again, with the familiar lack of success.

In speaking so much of our teaching, I ought not to leave the impression that the education section at Upavon was overburdened with work. Peter and I spent many pleasantly idle afternoons, chatting, drinking cups of coffee, glancing at the new books which had come in for the station library (also our responsibility) or simply gazing out of the window.

If this lotus-eating mode of existence became boring, then there was an officially-approved means of escape. Though Upavon was a headquarters station, therefore, by definition, a seat of bureaucracy, it did have attached to it a small aerodrome. This was used by the aircraft of the communications flights and also by the trainers—Chipmunks mostly—in which the officers of the flying branch kept up their necessary quota of flying hours. Ground officers were encouraged to take to the air as much as possible, and, if work seemed dull, it was quite all right to make one's escape into the sky, hitching a lift from whoever might be going up.

These joy-rides could be intensely exhilarating, with the whole of Wiltshire spread out beneath one, and the slender needle of Salisbury Cathedral spire rising in the distance, but they were seldom sedate. The younger pilots took pleasure in trying to frighten the groundhogs out of their wits. The splendidly manœuvrable little Chipmunks were thrown about the sky in loops, turns and mock dog-fights until one's stomach seemed to be left lingering several miles behind.

The one serious worry I might have had about these flights, though it never prevented me from asking for another ride, was the physical condition of some of those who piloted me. There were a small number of junior officers at Upavon who formed no part, either of headquarters staff, or of the service-station complement. They were with us on attachment. What this meant, most usually, was that they had been severely injured in crashes during training, and had been sent to us to await the verdict of the doctors, who would say whether or not they were physically fit to remain in the service. A wall-eye, a limp, hands with badly distorted or missing fingers—these were the marks that singled them out. Most had a rather desperate gaiety, a commitment to high-jinks and high spirits which served as a cover to what must have been their real feelings.

Understandably, it was the pilots in this group who were keenest to make use of the training facilities of the place, and who were the wildest in the aerobatics they performed. Every flight was a proof, even if no one who mattered was there to witness it, that flying skills were still theirs in full measure.

Yet one or two of them were also at pains to point out to me, as I climbed, perhaps rather pale, from the cockpit behind them, that these lively but in terms of actual speed very slow light aircraft were a very different proposition from the jets which fully active pilots flew. In military jets, notoriously, no slightest mistake or fumble was forgiven by the mechanism itself.

Brief forays in training aircraft over a small patch of south-west England were not the only flights I made. A month or two after I arrived at Upavon, I discovered from Peter that the station had a very important 'perk' reserved for its two education officers. In fact Upavon had an out-station, administratively united to it but physically separate. This, in itself, was not unusual. But this particular out-station happened to be situated in the south of France.

Transport Command maintained a small staging-post at the huge French military air base at Istres, which lay behind the Etang de Beirre, a marshy lagoon which itself lay slightly inland from Martigues. The unit there was much too small to have its own education officer, and therefore, to keep things within the framework of the regulations, one or other of us from Upavon had to spend a few days there at regular intervals. If nothing much got done on these trips, apart from a little careers guidance or educational counselling—no matter, the proprieties had been observed.

Peter was much less interested in 'abroad' than I was. He had already visited Istres, and, besides this, he was in love—an endemic condition with him, as I had rapidly discovered. Thus it was that, about six months after my conscription into the air force, I found myself flying southwards towards the sun. Our communications flight was still equipped with Ansons—a small twin-engined aircraft which went back, in design at least, to the middle thirties. We would make a leisurely journey to Istres, at extremely moderate height and speed. Because of prevailing weather conditions (being unpressurized, the Anson could not climb over a storm which lay in its path), we had decided to fly a semi-circular route, which made our progress yet more leisurely. We lunched in the Channel Islands, dined in Biarritz, then next morning flew along the line of the Pyrenees to our destination.

Istres was a small old-fashioned provincial town, with dusty squares and winding alleys. A statue of some pre-First-World-War radical politician adorned the main *place*; it may even have been Jean Jaurès. The inhabitants sat on wooden chairs outside the doors of their houses, watching the world go by.

If the town was small, the airbase was enormous; it was said to have the longest runways in Europe. Because of this, and because of its comparative isolation, the French had chosen to make it their main experimental centre. All sorts of strange products of French engineering ingenuity, as weird yet as logical as certain French cars, lay scattered about on the aprons, or were visible within the gaping doors of the enormous hangars. Conspicuous among them were the pick-a-back aircraft which had been the first to achieve manned supersonic flight—a small jet plane mounted on the back of a lumbering propeller-driven aircraft.

In the bustling mess, which served far better food than we ever tasted at home, amid a roar of talk and a clatter of thick white plates, the small group of English officers seemed very isolated. The French, it was said, regretted having given us a foothold on this top-secret base. A more likely reason was that, of all the officers who belonged to the English unit, only the CO spoke adequate French.

We visitors were greeted slightly less than cordially by our fellow-countrymen. The squadron leader in charge made edged jokes about people from command headquarters who came to France simply to get drunk and get in the way.

Had I had any illusions on the subject it would soon have been made plain to me that any formal attempts at 'education' on my part would be unwelcome. The unit was understaffed and working overtime. I could make myself available for consultation —that was all. Anxious not to be left hanging about, I asked if I could make myself useful in some other way, since my French was sufficient for most purposes. This suggestion was greeted with relief. Perhaps I would like to make a start straightaway by taking one of the corporals over to the French doctor?

The corporal turned out to be an outstandingly handsome man of about my own age. His spectacular good looks were highlighted by the fact that his hair was already completely grey. He complained of stomach pains, fever and a slightly loose bowel. Together we went to the surgery and I explained his symptoms. The doctor listened carefully then, with a vivid pantomime to reinforce what he was saying to me, he asked me to tell the patient to remove his trousers and underpants. Obediently, but clearly somewhat puzzled—as was I—the corporal did so. Immediately, the doctor produced one of those huge rectal thermometers favoured by the French medical profession. When my companion realized what was to be done to him a deep blush appeared on his face. A moment later the same blush could be seen appearing below the tails of his shirt.

To make matters worse, the doctor then announced that he intended to prescribe suppositories, which would soon deal with the symptoms complained of. Another and even deeper blush could not disguise the mulishness of the corporal's expression. The suppositories, it was clear, would be thrown away the instant he got back to his own quarters.

That evening we visitors began to discuss what we should do with our free time. A visit to the local brothel was jokingly canvassed, but it was decided to settle for dinner and a bit of quiet drinking instead. We ate strongly flavoured Provençal food at a little restaurant in the main *place*, just beside the gesticulating statue I have already mentioned. It was at this juncture that the women materialized. Nobody seemed to know quite who had invited them to join us, but at any rate it was clear that they were known to the officers of the Istres unit, two or three of whom were dining with us. It seemed to me that the residents greeted the ladies with reserve. After dinner, at any rate, they rapidly excused themselves. We were left with our new friends—three of them to five of us.

It was now suggested that we move on to 'a sort of nightclub'. This turned out to be a house which was almost, but not quite, like a private residence, done up in dusty velvets, filled with

awkward lumps of oak furniture, but nevertheless with the echo-
ing tiled floors of the region. Nobody else was there. The owner/
proprietor hovered, offering drinks at high prices. What could we
have? 'Oh, almost anything.' Mindful of the unit commander's
tirade against drunkenness, I opted for Fernet-Branca. If it cured
hangovers, as it was supposed to, then surely it would prevent
them too?

As the member of our group with the most French, I was
pressed into service as interpreter. Compliments were paid. The
drinks came. Glances were exchanged. A game of poker-dice was
proposed. The man who lost would pay for whatever drinks
were then outstanding. The woman who lost—well, perhaps a
kiss would be enough? Early in the proceedings, I won, and
leaned rather self-consciously towards the most attractive of the
ladies. She was pale, with a full face, and a slight double-chin.
Her lips were cherry-red and glossy, in the fashion of the time.
She seized me firmly and an extremely active tongue was thrust
into my mouth. The older men watched me sardonically.

Later, at a lull in the game, I asked her if she had always lived
in Istres. There was a moment's hesitation. 'No,' she said. 'My
husband works here for the government, but at present he has
business in Paris.'

I had by this time swallowed quite a number of little glasses of
Fernet-Branca, and was beginning to feel queasy. I took another
sip of the bitter drink and a cold sweat suddenly began to trickle
from forehead and upper lip. My services as interpreter were, in
any case, no longer needed. It was time to slip away.

I came down to coffee and croissants the next morning with
my feeling of queasiness greatly intensified. Only one of my
companions was awaiting me at the table in the hotel garden
where *petit déjeuner* was set out. He, I recollected, was the one
who had announced his engagement the week before. He took
on my appearance with a broad grin. Neither of us made any
reference to the events of the previous evening.

I spent the rest of the morning doing my best to hide my condition. As long as I was on my feet, and hard at work, nothing
would be said. When lunch-time was near it was announced that
a vehicle would be taking off-duty members of the unit to a

nearby beach, in order to bathe. Would we like to go along? Only
I was free to accept—it seemed as good a way as any of removing
myself from the scrutiny of the CO. All morning his eyes had
been fixed on me speculatively.

Aboard the bus I found the handsome corporal, now apparently
fully recovered. I was the only officer present, and an educa-
tionist and a National Serviceman to boot. It was tacitly assumed
that rank could be forgotten. Conversation flowed idly along.
'I hear that Wing Co. you brought with you was around with old
Madeleine last night,' the corporal remarked suddenly. I realized
that he was referring to the best-looking of the women we had
met the night before. 'Well, Red here,' jerking his elbow towards
another corporal, ugly but conspicuously muscular, who was
lounging across the aisle from us, 'used to fuck her regularly a
while back. Lasted about six months. Said she was a bit of a
handful, even for him.'

Apparently the impression I made at Istres, despite the Fernet-
Branca, was not too disastrous. It was indicated that I should not
be unwelcome if I came again, and in fact I paid several more
visits to the unit.

The most memorable of these was the journey on which our
Anson burst a tyre when landing at the French military airport
at Dijon. The accident had marvellous consequences. For three
days we ate and drank while we waited for a replacement wheel
to be flown out to us. Generous at any rate in this, the government made ample allowances to officers temporarily on service
abroad. One night, after a magnificent meal and a splendid bottle
of wine, both of them courtesy of the British taxpayer, I wandered
out into the streets of the town. Almost at once I came upon a
theatre, its architecture based upon that of the Roman temple at
Nîmes. A performance was just about to begin, and people were
pouring through the doors under its portico. The play adver-
tised on the posters was Sartre's *Kean*, and the leading rôle was
to be taken by Pierre Brasseur. On impulse, I went to the box
office and asked for a ticket. A single *strapontin* was left. For the
next three hours I sat, or, rather, nodded, through Sartre's
romantic play. Its rhetoric mingled with the fumes of the wine
I had drunk, until I didn't know if the drama was being enacted

inside or outside my head; in the theatre of the brain, or in the real and physical theatre, which was very like those that Kean himself must have played in. It was the most unexpected bonus of my time as a conscript.

Not that the theatre was always so kind to me during my time in the RAF. In addition to going to plays whenever I could—on this one occasion in Dijon, or as often as I could manage it in London—I had become heavily involved with amateur dramatics on camp. I no longer had many illusions about my own histrionic capacities; but putting on plays was a way, in the first place, of alleviating the boredom of our isolated circumstances, and in the second place it helped to bring officers and other ranks together. The service, as always, took an ambiguous attitude towards this mingling of the two sides. Amateur dramatics were an officially approved form of leisure activity, and there were even competitions between various stations in the district. On the other hand it was difficult to gauge what degree of fraternization service custom permitted.

Since I was officially in charge of the productions we put on, the social stresses fell upon me. What was I to do when our leading man—a National Service AC2 with a place at university waiting for him—fell in love with a wing commander's daughter? More ticklish still, what was I to say in order to placate our leading lady, a flashing beauty in the Spanish style, married to a warrant officer, who all too easily took umbrage at the attitudes and manners of our young WRAF officers?

On one occasion, the strain of running a production, and at the same time keeping the peace, proved too much. After the last performance of *Worm's Eye View*, in which I played Sidney, the termagant landlady's creepy son, a rather tense cast party took place. In a fit of absence of mind, I drank a couple of tumblerfuls of neat gin. Since I had eaten nothing for most of the previous week, the alcohol knocked me cold, not at the party itself, but as I was on my way back to my quarters. Luckily, it was an election-night, and one of my brother officers, who had stayed up late to watch the results on television, stumbled over my body on his way to bed. By this time it was raining hard, and I was soaked and suffering from loss of body heat. I woke up twenty-four hours later in the camp infirmary, wondering what had happened to me. The doctor rescued me from what might have been an embarrassing interview with the CO by announcing that he was convinced that someone must have slipped me a Mickey Finn.

On the whole, however, service life in England settled into a routine. As the months went by, the work of the education section tended more and more to fall into my hands. Peter had a long bout of ill-health, and, in addition to this, he was now more seriously in love than ever before. His 'little bunny', as he always referred to her, filled his thoughts to the exclusion of everything else. When he wasn't out with her, or on the phone to her, he was talking about her—hands clasped behind his head, legs propped on the desk. His clerk and I got on with things as best we could, while the amorous monologue washed over us.

Some jobs were admittedly a trifle tedious. We were perpetually engaged in stock-takings of one kind or another—checking the contents of the library or those of some station store. The library inventory had been fudged so often, by successive education officers, that there was no alternative but to fudge it again. One store, for some reason long unopened and therefore uninspected, turned out to hold thousands of little cardboard boxes, each containing either a crystal or a valve for a different mark of service radio. There were scores, perhaps hundreds, of different types. Many must have been long obsolete. All had to be checked against an enormous list. After three dusty, sweaty days, during which my actual totals diverged more and more widely from what should have been on the shelves in theory, I decided to call a halt. This inventory must be fudged too.

It was all too easy to fall victim to the prevailing *laisser aller*. The life I had lived at university, and the friends I had made there, seemed increasingly remote. While I was at Jurby, Oscar Mellor had produced a pamphlet of my poems in his Fantasy Press series: the arrangement had been made before I went down. It seemed very strange to open the parcel there on the Isle of Man. I could scarcely believe that it was I who had written these verses. My first publication did not stir me as it is supposed to stir most people.

F

Jurby gave me little opportunity to write, but even after I arrived at Upavon I produced very few poems, and I knew that these were not as good as those I had been writing during my last year as an undergraduate. It was easier to spend my evenings playing bridge in the mess, rather than struggling with pen and paper in my room. Not that my bridge was always appreciated. My regular partner, one of the senior civil servants who came down from the Air Ministry to see us, several days a week, finally exploded when I bid us into a small slam and won it by playing every finesse the wrong way round. As the last card fell he surged to his feet and bellowed, 'You had no right to win that, partner!' Then he stamped from the room. Our difference was soon made up, but I played bridge less often thereafter. Gradually and insidiously, however, the RAF had become the devil I knew; it provided me with a sheltered, easy, perfectly regular existence. There had been one person whom I saw nearly every week-end in London. We would talk—and mostly quarrel—for hours in her small flat behind Marble Arch, despairingly looking for a way to deepen a relationship which, though pleasant enough, was spoilt by impatience on her part and an insensitive complacency on mine. But suddenly it was over—she had decided to marry, and to marry somebody else. Upavon became, not a place to get away from, but a refuge from this disappointment. I became more and more absorbed in the welfare side of an education officer's work. I could even say, with a show of truth, that the RAF enabled me to do some good in the world.

I was on camp, one summer week-end, it being my turn to serve as station duty officer. In the morning, a group of local farmers, armed with shot-guns, had come to the great oak-tree which stood beside the mess. Many rooks nested there; the air was always filled with their cawing. Methodically, our visitors shot them out of the tree. The glossy black bodies flapped like wet rags to the grass, tipping some of the blades with drops of blood. Unreasonably disturbed by this incident, I had gone to bed in the afternoon. Suddenly, after sleeping for a couple of hours, I sat up, rubbed the glue from my eyes, took my portable type-writer out of its case and began to write the first of a score of letters to prospective employers.

CHAPTER NINETEEN

THE PLACE WHERE I ended up was a London advertising agency—but that is a topic which does not belong to this book. There are, however, two subjects of different but related kinds which may serve to conclude my interim report, two areas of activity where I continued the prolonged process of growing up. One of these was poetry and the other was art-criticism.

The story of my growing-up in poetry is largely connected with the history of the Group, once upon a time highly controversial, and now, I notice, on the verge of becoming 'historic', like one of those second-rate Victorian country houses the impoverished owners throw open to visitors, in imitation of Woburn and Chatsworth. The University of Reading devoted an exhibition to the Group last year.

I was not its founder. That honour belongs to Philip Hobsbaum. Philip had been an undergraduate at Cambridge, reading English at Downing, while I was studying history at Oxford. He saw one of my poems in an undergraduate magazine, liked it, and wrote to me about it. This was a very special kind of honour, and I was appropriately flattered. We Oxford poets had an inferiority complex about our Cambridge contemporaries. The chief cause was Thom Gunn. Though his first collection, *Fighting Terms*, did not appear until 1954, the poems he was publishing in magazines were already much discussed, and were causing ripples in a literary world well beyond our own student environment.

It is not difficult to explain the immediate success that Gunn's early poems enjoyed. A Cambridge passion for Eng. Lit. was combined with a rather taking bully-boy strut; aggressive phrases and rhythms strained, but never broke, the boundaries of conventional forms:

Hacks in the Fleet and nobles in the Tower.
Shakespeare must keep the peace, and Jonson's thumb
Be branded (for manslaughter), in the power
Of irons lay the admired Southampton.
Above all swayed the diseased and doubtful queen:
Her state canopied by the glamour of pain.*

In the circumstances of the time it was a heady mixture. In Gunn's work, the meritocrats found a new day-dream—that of the academic as man of action. In due course, this was to have a considerable effect on the development of British poetry in general.

However, it turned out that Philip was not an admirer of Gunn. He was eager to introduce me to the work of two Cambridge poets whose work I had not as yet heard of: Ted Hughes and Peter Redgrove. But, more important than this, he was hoping to put into practice an idea he had derived from working with Dr Leavis.

This emerged when at last we met each other—I think I had not as yet left the RAF, but was just about to obtain my discharge. He told me that he was planning to run a series of literary evenings at his flat near Marble Arch, and asked me to come along to them.

I had never been very comfortable at literary gatherings in Oxford. I always felt my energy as a party-goer made me suspect, and, indeed, I think it did. Much later, at about the time when I published my second book of poems, and when I was already making a small reputation as a journalist, an old friend of those days—also a poet—turned to me guilelessly and said (we had been talking about Oxford): 'Whoever would have thought that you would come to anything, Teddy?' I understood that he meant the question as a compliment, but it was hard to frame a reply.

Philip cared nothing for all this. He only knew me by correspondence. He wanted me to come to the discussion group he planned because he had liked one or two of my poems. That, for him, was introduction enough. And I agreed to go along, despite

* From the poem 'A Mirror for Poets' in *Fighting Terms* by Thom Gunn (Faber & Faber, 1962).

my initial reservations, because I felt cut off from London, and cut off from contemporary poetry, by the two years I had spent in the forces.

Philip's plan was very simple. He planned to base himself on Dr Leavis's teaching methods, but to apply these to the work of his contemporaries. A text would be put in front of us, and we would be asked to react to it, and to discuss it as candidly as we liked. In addition to the fact that the work would be new, with nothing known about it from previous report or experience, there would be another significant deviation from university practice. The discussion group would be a complete democracy. The moderator would undertake a purely technical function —that of keeping the discussion going on reasonably coherent lines—but there would be no question of him putting himself above the rest.

The plan worked, rather to my surprise. Though the early meetings of the group were disorderly, in comparison to the more typical sessions which came later, those of us who came regularly found that we were becoming deeply involved in these weekly gatherings, and that surprisingly much came out of them. Most of the credit belonged to Philip. He had a number of qualities, some intellectual and some physical, which made him a good chairman. He was fond of argument in the way that other men are fond of food. He got enormous enjoyment from its twists and turns, while at the same time he had no patience with slipshod thinking or intellectual evasiveness. The fact that he had, at that time, no poetic ambitions himself, but intended to concentrate on writing novels, made him acceptable to the rest of us. Often he seemed impatient, and inclined to hector and browbeat, and the disputes would often grow noisy and acrimonious. But the forcefulness of his manner concealed a respect for intellectual democracy which he carried very far. He said, and really seemed to believe, that almost anyone had it in them to write a good poem, if only they could be persuaded to ask themselves the right questions. For a long time I too tried to make this proposition an article of faith. The fact that I can no longer do so argues, perhaps, for a loss of confidence in the possibilities offered by poetry, rather than for a loss of confidence in human nature. Finally, there was the fact that Philip was a marvellous reader, with an exceptionally beautiful voice. In the course of a discussion he would lavish prodigies of skill on an apparently feeble and hopeless text; and it was these readings which often persuaded us to look again at something we had felt inclined to dismiss out of hand.

Gradually, during its first year of operation, the discussion group evolved an agreed method of operation. For example, each meeting would be devoted to the work of one writer, as this seemed to provide a much greater continuity of discussion. And, since the work was to be cyclostyled, so that everyone could have a copy of the text in his or her hand, then it seemed better to have it ready the week beforehand. Those who came to a particular meeting could take next week's sheet away with them. To the others, it would be sent by post. Gradually the mailing-list grew, until the 'song-sheets', as they were called, achieved the status of an informal (and free) poetry magazine. But this was a long time later.

The composition of the discussion group itself was very various. Philip brought in his university crony Peter Redgrove, whose work he greatly admired; and there were readings, in the early days, of poems Ted Hughes sent over from America, where he was then teaching. Peter and Ted had both attended similar, but less ambitious, readings organized by Philip at Cambridge. Ted's poems, in particular, soon acquired totemic value with us. Yet another recruit from Cambridge was the Canadian poet, David Wevill, whose poems shared an expressionist character with those of Hughes and Redgrove.

Meanwhile, I brought in some of the poets I had known at Oxford, notably George MacBeth and Alan Brownjohn. But, despite the fact that the meetings had been started on the basis of university experience, and despite the number of recent Oxbridge graduates who came to them, the Group (for it now seems reasonable to award it a capital letter) soon took on an anti-academic tinge. Some of the most important of the members had not been to either Oxford or Cambridge, and a few had no university education at all. Martin Bell, older than the rest of us, had read English at University College, Southampton, and had then served in the Royal Engineers throughout the war. He was now working as a teacher. A chance meeting with Redgrove (they lived in the same suburb) had brought him back to poetry, after many years of not writing verse. Another important recruit was a young Australian, Peter Porter, then working as an assistant in an Oxford Street bookshop.

One striking feature of the Group, especially if one looks at the list of poets whose work is included in *A Group Anthology*—this, published in 1963, represents a rather later stage in our evolution —is the large number of members who were born abroad. In addition to a Canadian, an Australian and a Jamaican (myself), there are Taner Baybars, who is a Cypriot Turk, and the Pakistani writer Zulfikhar Ghose. Another oddity of the Group's composition, less easily detectable until one had met the bulk of the regular membership, was that few of the leading lights had done National Service. Some had been exempted on medical grounds—Hobsbaum himself, for example, suffered from very poor eyesight—and some had not been liable because of their Commonwealth citizenship.

It was factors such as these which helped to mould the Group into something more than the sum of its parts. As the weekly meetings continued—they were soon moved to a flat Philip and his wife rented in a strange, leafy enclave in Stockwell—the Group became a living entity, with a character of its own. In part, that character reflected the times. In part, it was an expression of our separate personalities and backgrounds, and of the way in which these reacted upon and modified each other. And in part it grew from the methods we used.

The late fifties were a period of rumbling discontent among intellectuals. Their disaffection made a sharp contrast to the prosperous complacency of the rest of the country. The mood is one that people now connect with the theatre, and particularly with Osborne's *Look Back in Anger*, which burst on the London theatre-going public in the year after the Group was formed. The symposium *Declaration*, published in October 1957, was also a good guide to the prevailing mood. Here, too, Osborne's impatient voice rang out: 'Are we going to continue to be fooled by a class of inept deceivers, are we going to go on being ruled by them? They *are* inept and they always have been because they are incapable of recognizing a problem.'*

None of the Group poets had ambitions to be a playwright —at least that I can remember. And none of us was sufficiently well known to be asked to contribute to *Declaration*. We were, however, affected by what was being done and said by our contemporaries. The impact which this outburst of intellectual protest had upon us was modified by our own personal circumstances. I have mentioned, for instance, that when I came to London I got a job in an advertising agency. Redgrove was also in advertising—his father was prominent in the profession. Later, Peter Porter was to leave his bookshop and become a copywriter. At one time, he, Redgrove and I all worked for the same firm.

Advertising was one of the great bugbears of the new rebels —they blamed it for the corruption and the complacency of the society they wanted to scrap. For them, it was a cause, not a symptom. We, making a modest living by it, were inclined to take the opposite view. When the Group became both well known and unpopular (as we shall see, it had a success which aroused a great deal of jealousy), this connection with advertising was one of the reproaches which was most regularly flung at our heads. We were, all of us, 'copywriter poets', just as the poets grouped under the banner of the Movement could never shake off the label 'academic'.

What advertising experience did was to make us acknowledge, not only the appetites and the customs, but the characteristic imagery of the urban society that surrounded us. This was most conspicuously true of the work of Peter Porter. Porter, when he first read to the Group, had been one of those young poets who are the despair of critics because they write in an elliptical private language, too confident of their own intelligence to state the obvious. He, blinking at us through his horn-rimmed glasses, was taken aback by our vehement refusal to understand phrases and sentences which seemed to him perfectly clear. But gradually his work came into focus:

* *Declaration*, edited by Tom Maschler (Cape, 1957).

This new Daks suit, greeny-brown,
Oyster coloured buttons, single vent, tapered
Trousers, no waistcoat, hairy tweed—my own:
A suit to show responsibility, to show
Return to life—easily got for two pounds down
Paid off in six months—the first stage of the change.
I am only the image I can force upon the town.*

The 'coming into focus' was, of course, a twofold process. The poet became less cryptic; the audience learned to stretch their own capacities, in order to absorb the new things he was trying to say.

Our mutual bias was, in any case, not only towards clarity, but towards concreteness. Looking at *A Group Anthology* now, I am struck, to use an art critic's term, by the naturalism of its contents. This tendency was made the more emphatic by the fact that many of us soon started to experiment with the dramatic monologue. The reason for this was the circumstances in which we found ourselves. The Group provided every poet who attended it with an audience he could envisage—not solitary readers unknown to him, not a sea of faces in a vague 'out there', but a roomful of people with familiar personalities. Using the dramatic monologue was a way of speaking out, and yet of preserving a screen between oneself and these friends whom one knew perhaps too intimately. Reading poems aloud encouraged the use of colloquial language, and the deliberate creation of some character or personality, separate from oneself, as a vehicle for what one wanted to say.

Oddly enough, we arrived at the dramatic monologue before we came to Browning. But what we were doing did suggest, at least to me, that Browning would be a good poet to look at. Some of the long poems I wrote at a time when the Group was fully established—monologues put into the mouths of painters such as Rubens and Caravaggio—were undoubtedly the most Browningesque products of our joint enterprise. Yet it was also a reading of Browning which suggested to me the first doubts about what we were doing. The inclusiveness of the great

* From the poem 'Metamorphosis' in *Once Bitten*, *Twice Bitten* by Peter Porter (Scorpion Press, 1961).

Victorians contrasted with our own exclusiveness, particularly with regard to any poetry not written in English.

Of course, a little influence filtered in from French—Redgrove made some variations on Rimbaud's prose-poems, which seemed to attract him chiefly because of the violence of their imagery; Martin Bell wrote transpositions of Laforgue; Alan Brownjohn's adaptation of a poem by Prévert, 'We are going to see the rabbit', appears in *A Group Anthology*. But none of this showed any real curiosity about what French poets might be writing contemporaneously with ourselves. The Group played no real part in the birth of the translation movement which flourished in the sixties, though a number of individual Group poets followed in its wake.

Something ought also to be said about the political isolation of the Group. Since it was founded and flourished just in the days when the New Left was at its height, and when CND polarized the emotions and the energy of many writers (the first Aldermaston March took place at Easter 1958), one might have expected to find a political overtone in our discussions. One might also have thought that many directly political poems would be read at our evenings. This was not the case. A poem like Alan Brownjohn's 'William Empson at Aldermaston' was the exception rather than the rule.

What did flavour our poetry was a general sense of the terror of the times. It emerged most strongly, perhaps, in some of Redgrove's fantasies, and in the poetry of MacBeth and Porter. Porter's work was often leavened with a sardonic humour which made it memorable:

> London is full of chickens on electric spits,
>   Cooking in windows where the public pass.
> This, say the chickens, is their Auschwitz,
>   And all poetry eaters are psychopaths.*

MacBeth's horrors, more often than not, had a *grand guignol* element which made it hard to be certain how seriously he meant them to be taken.

I have wondered, since, if the ambiguity of MacBeth's writing,

* From 'Metamorphosis' in Peter Porter's *Once Bitten, Twice Bitten*.

now latent, now overt, wasn't his form of defence to the psychic pressures which the Group put on all of us. In those days 'group therapy' wasn't the fashionable concept it has now become; and my feeling is that we were remarkably innocent about psychology, and not especially interested in it. Yet it was inevitable that a discussion of the faults to be found in the poem should touch, at least by implication, on the flaws to be found in the person. The great emphasis we put, largely thanks to Philip, in both clarity of intention as well as clarity of expression, often led us towards dangerous areas. Since the poem itself had often been written to purge or reconcile some conflict, it could sometimes only be criticized by pointing out that the purgation was incomplete, or that the battle was being fought on the wrong ground. A discussion might sometimes become a collective effort, on the part of the rest of us, to force the poet whose work was under discussion that night to acknowledge some characteristic which we all saw in him, and which he was determined to deny. Such discussions required great skill on the part of the moderator if they were not to become personal slanging matches. They also required, and still more urgently, a mutual trustfulness. When I look back on the Group, I think this is the aspect of it which I remember with the greatest nostalgia. In some curious way we really did manage to trust one another not to use the information which the poems and discussions provided in ways which might be hurtful. If one considers the vanity and egotism of young writers—and few of us were exempt—this candour was surprising.

Since the Group lasted for such a long period—it flourished for ten years, first under Philip's chairmanship and then under mine, it would be surprising if one did not recall disadvantages and flaws, as well as what was good about it. Of all the disadvantages, the most crucial, and perhaps the least expected by us when we began—but then we were all idealists—turned out to be the inflexibility of the personalities involved. After some years of regular meetings, it was possible to anticipate nearly all the arguments which would be produced for or against a particular poem, and sometimes, even, the very phrases which would be uttered in the course of the discussion.

For the newcomer, who heard his poems discussed for the first time, the procedure remained fascinating. Even if the verdict was unfavourable, a young poet found it flattering to be the focus of such concentrated attention, on the part of men who were, by this time, extremely fluent controversialists. For the old hands, I suspect, the discussions grew gradually, and perhaps imperceptibly, less valuable. All too often I found that I was listening, not to the argument itself, but to the undercurrent, seeking a hint of a reaction which was unexpected or not according to rule. In the final years of my chairmanship, I took a lot of trouble to seek out recruits who, I hoped. would rebel against the prevailing orthodoxies. All too often, I would be drawn aside at the end of the evening, and asked why I had invited 'that dreadful man', who was so clearly out of sympathy with everything we stood for.

As one might expect, the Group was not the only thing of its kind which flourished in London at that period. A number of us also went to the gatherings which G. S. Fraser, who had now left the *New Statesman* for the *Times Literary Supplement*, held at his flat in Beaufort Street. The atmosphere there was rather different.

At the Group, alcohol on the premises was banned, though anyone with a thirst could slip out to the pub in the interval which came halfway through the proceedings. By outsiders, this rule of ours was much mocked, and when the Group began to attract publicity, we would find ourselves characterized as a band of severely puritan teetotallers.

Arriving at George Fraser's flat, one discovered that an immense bottle party was in progress. The room was filled with smoke and noise, and new arrivals were constantly pushing their way in. While his wife Paddy opened the door and welcomed newcomers, George would try to maintain some kind of order, asking those who had brought manuscripts to read them in turn. After the reading he would ask for comments. If these came from the Scottish poet Burns Singer, who functioned as a kind of resident gadfly, uproar would break out, which the host vainly attempted to still by passing round further supplies of beer and wine.

If Singer's fierce tongue was a disruptive factor, so too was the attitude of Group members. Though we were nearly all of us

poor and struggling, we felt no attraction towards the old
Bohemia of the forties, which we identified with some of the
other poets present. Our usual way of baiting the company was
for one or other of us to read a poem by Ted Hughes. A favourite
was 'The Martyrdom of Bishop Farrar', later to be the final item
in Ted's first book, *The Hawk in the Rain:*

> The sullen-jowled watching Welsh townspeople
> Hear him crack in the fire's mouth; they see what
> Black oozing twist of stuff bubbles the smell
> That tars and retches their lungs: no pulpit
> Of his ever held their eyes so still,
> Never, as now his agony, his wit.*

Perhaps because his talent was on the very threshold of an
acceptance which would alter the existing poetic geography,
opposition to what Hughes did was, at this moment, and in this
circle, especially fierce.

But there were lighter moments than this at George's gatherings. Who could forget, for example, the middle-aged poet who
read an interminable poem about Simla in a mournful and barely
audible voice? The poem showed an obsession with exact topo-
graphy—the two lines I remember ran:

> The streets run up and down,
> And the streets run across and across

When the poem ended, a total, and for the place and circumstances, totally exceptional, silence fell. George, whose kindness
and good nature were and are legendary, pulled himself together
and uttered a few rather subdued compliments. Instead of being
placated by these, the indignant poet burst out with: 'You say
that, George. Yet you never print my poems in the *Times
Literary Supplement*. Why don't you print this one, George?'
Whereupon another and even deeper silence fell.

Our collective appearances at George's bottle-parties were,

* From the poem 'The Martyrdom of Bishop Farrar' in *The Hawk
in the Rain* by Ted Hughes (Faber & Faber, 1957).

perhaps, the thing which first began to get the Group talked about. We were soon to realize that the rest of the literary world viewed us in no very favourable light. There are certain conventions which a young poet flouts at his peril—and one of these is the convention of individuality. The Movement poets had obeyed it by resisting the Movement label; by saying, frequently, that they felt they had little in common with one another. The members of the Group, on the other hand, could not deny their own inter-connection. Indeed, to outsiders, it must have seemed that they boasted of it. We made things worse because we were not modest. The outspokenness we had developed in private soon became a weapon which we employed in public.

Meanwhile, some of the more prominent members of the Group were publishing their first collections of poetry; and the literary situation itself was changing round us. Peter Redgrove's *The Collector* appeared early in 1960; Peter Porter's *Once Bitten, Twice Bitten* and my own *A Tropical Childhood* came out in 1961. Had these books been published a little earlier, they would have seemed—at least in the case of Porter and Redgrove—a direct and calculated riposte to the Movement poets. But already things were becoming more complicated.

It seems to me now that there are times when the little world which is interested in poetry lives with great intensity, and times when it scarcely lives at all. The end of the fifties and the beginning of the sixties was a period of intensity. In 1957 Ted Hughes's first book, *The Hawk in the Rain*, came out. Rarely has a first volume of poems had such an overwhelming success. In 1959, Faber published the first English edition of Robert Lowell's *Life Studies*. This was to have a greater influence on the fortunes of English poetry and poets than anything written by Hughes, though anyone energetic enough to look up the reviews which *Life Studies* got at the time will find them strangely hesitant, if one considers Lowell's later reputation with English critics. Poets were quicker to hail his change of style. I remember, for example, that Peter Porter and I wrote a brash and indignant letter to the *Spectator* about the lukewarm welcome which their critic gave to the book. Soon enough, Lowell was to be used as a stick with which to beat both of us.

One curious thing about Ted Hughes's work, considering both its impact and its intrinsic quality, has been its barrenness. Hughes could electrify the poetry-reading public, but was unable to fertilize other poets, even those, like ourselves, who were his earliest admirers. There is no true 'school of Hughes', only a scattering of more or less slavish imitators. What he did revive, in the minds of his readers and still more so in the minds of those who came into contact with him after his American visit, was the idea of the poet as a heroic being, who belonged to a different kind of moral order:

> I climbed through woods in the hour-before-dawn dark.
> Evil air, a frost-making stillness,
> Not a leaf, not a bird,—
> A world cast in frost. I came out above the wood
> Where my breath left tortuous statues in the iron light.
> But the valleys were draining the darkness . . .*

Listening to him perform at a public reading, one felt oneself to be in the presence of a modern Byron.

Lowell, who, thanks to the degree of self-exposure to be discovered in his poetry, might have been thought of as the more genuinely Byronic figure, fulfilled a different function. The cult of his poetry which sprang up in England was, primarily, an expression of English feelings about what was happening to natively English literature. The most powerful expression of these feelings is to be found in the Preface which A. Alvarez wrote for his Penguin anthology *The New Poetry*, published in 1962, and soon to become the bible of a new generation of poetry-readers. In this Preface, Alvarez launched an attack on what he called 'the gentility principle'. 'My own feeling,' he concluded, 'is that a good deal of poetic talent exists in England at the moment. But whether or not it will come to anything depends not on the machinations of any literary racket but on the degree to which the poets can remain immune to the disease so often found in English culture: gentility.'

* From the poem 'The Horses' in Ted Hughes's *The Hawk in the Rain*.

The choice of poems in Alvarez's book exemplifies his ideas in what I feel to be an eccentric way. A small group of Americans —Lowell, John Berryman, Anne Sexton—is followed by a somewhat larger selection of contemporary English poets, most of them associated with the Movement. 'Gentility', one might have thought, was one of the things Movement poetry was about —in technique, at least, if not in content.

However, the chief consequence of Alvarez's anthology was a surge of enthusiasm for so-called 'confessional verse'. Confessional verse was stringently defined. It had to be of American origin. English writers with distinctly 'confessional' tendencies—they range from Martin Bell to Elizabeth Jennings—were either ignored or else dismissed as 'embarrassing'. What fascinated English critics, all of a sudden, was Freudian rhetoric, the monologue from the analyst's couch. Yet they never seemed to recognize how much the technique had been honed by encounters with psychiatry; they never remarked on the mask—that of the patient undergoing analysis—which the American poet often wore over his more usual and everyday face. It was as if, in paying homage to forthright personal poetry of this type, the English were, at the same time, making a masochistic acknowledgement of the superiority of American literature. Just as Britain was, in the world of international politics, inexorably losing the importance she had once possessed; so too, it began to be assumed that American poetry was automatically superior to anything being written in England.

As they emerged into a more public arena, with the publication of *A Group Anthology* in 1963, the Group poets bore the brunt of this assumption, just as they suffered by comparison with Hughes's glamour. The collection did not receive nearly such a good press as Conquest's *New Lines*, which had preceded it by eight years, though it is worth noting that a number of the contributors were soon tacitly accepted as writers who deserved attention.

Yet I must now admit that the publication of the anthology marks, in my own mind, the point at which the Group started to decline. The hostility aroused by the book—on the one hand by those who felt it threatened an established orthodoxy, and on the other by those who thought it was not adventurous enough—was a minor matter. And the furious protests of those who scented a cabal would soon die down. What did the damage was success. The publicity generated by the book brought in more and more recruits. Meetings in my two small rooms in Sydney Street were packed to suffocation, Friday after Friday. In such circumstances, the quality of the discussions could only go down. It fell, first, because there were now too many people present for the old intimacy to be maintained; and second, because there were too many aspiring poets who wanted to read, which meant that we lost our former sense of continuity.

But there was another problem as well, less to do with the Group in particular than with the position of the poet in England. Thanks to the Penguin Modern Poets series (financed by the money earned from the paperback edition of *Lady Chatterley*) contemporary poetry reached a wider and wider audience in England during the sixties. This tempted poets to think of themselves as professionals, in the sense that there were already professional painters and professional musicians. We, in the Group, were not exempt from this feeling. And we were growing older. Faced with the problem, not only of self-definition, but of what we were to do for a living, we chose different solutions. Some of us, as I have said, worked for a while in advertising, but never with any great faith in this as a permanent way of life. Some went to the universities (in spite of everything); one to an art-school; MacBeth continued his career in the BBC. More crucial than the precise source of income was the vision which each poet had of himself. Some saw poetry as a primary activity, which another occupation must sustain. A few, with the upsurge of Pop poetry, saw the poet's rôle as being to occupy the Tom Tiddler's ground between the guru and the entertainer. My own reactions were different. I could not accept either of these as the solution.

As the years went by, as the Group continued to meet under my chairmanship, I was faced with a number of problems. One was to do with judgement, and I can locate it in a quotation from Northrop Frye. 'The sense of value,' he says, 'is an individual, unpredictable, variable, incommunicable, indemonstrable, and mainly intuitive reaction to knowledge. In knowledge, the context of the work of literature is literature; in value-judgement,

the context of the work of literature is the reader's experience.'*
My judgement was now being increasingly influenced by experience of modern art, through my practice as a critic. This
opened a gap in communication with most of those who came
to my house on Friday evenings.

More important, there was my own view of myself and what
I was doing, now changing to something which I thought the
other members of the Group might not find sympathetic. I did
not want to be a professional poet, though I did want to be a
professional writer—an ambition I had now gone some distance
towards achieving, and which I was eventually to fulfil. For me,
poetry was becoming, not so much a process of making or of
communication, but a deliberate act of self-discovery. The poem,
by insisting on finding its own shape, its own imagery, its own
system of inclusions and omissions, could often reveal to me that
what I did feel was in fact different from what I thought I felt.

I came to think of my poetry as being like a stream which
flowed through the kind of limestone country I had known as a
child in Jamaica. At times it flowed murmuring and hidden, in a
way that only I was aware of, a faint whisper in some remote
hollow of the brain. At other times it burst upwards, and could
be seen rushing along in the light, deep or shallow according to
the lie of the land. I hoped that, like those Jamaican streams, it
ran direct and clear, but for the time at least I began to find
arguments about technique irrelevant. And arguments about
content were positively unhelpful, because more and more I
wanted this to choose itself, unprompted by my own or any other
consciousness, as an expression of the dialogue I heard at all times
going on within me.

Though I was now a skilful chairman, I felt dishonest when I
exercised these skills every Friday evening, while hugging to
myself the knowledge of my own reservations, and of the fact
that my submission to the democracy Philip had insisted on from
the start was only external. In the circumstances, and after ten
good years, it seemed to me time to call a halt.

* From the essay 'On Value Judgements' in *The Stubborn Structure*
by Northrop Frye (Methuen, 1970).

CHAPTER TWENTY

IN FRANCE, EVER since Baudelaire, it has been assumed that poetry and art-criticism go together, and that the poet and the artist are natural allies in support of the modernist ideal. No such assumption can be made in England. I would go so far as to say that, since Pound and Eliot, poets in England have been afraid of conscious avant-gardism and indeed of international modernism. Auden's loss of nerve over *The Orators*, Dylan Thomas's hostility to any suggestion that he had been influenced by the surrealists, are examples of this. The poets of the Group, with whom I associated, were no exception to the rule. When, for example, Oliver Bernard read some of his Apollinaire translations to us, at the time when we still met in Stockwell, the evening was a dismal failure. We found the content of the poems either incomprehensible or silly.

Where poetry itself was concerned, avant-gardism, having found no welcome in London, struggled to take root in the provinces. But at the Group our view of poetry tended to be almost as London-centred as that of the critics who wrote for the *New Statesman* and the *Times Literary Supplement*. The only information which got through the barrier we had put up around ourselves was that sent us by Hobsbaum from his various places of residence. Moving first to Sheffield, then to Belfast, and finally to Glasgow, he seemed to find young poets wherever he went. I first saw the work of Seamus Heaney, for instance, on a duplicated sheet which Philip sent me from Belfast. But I and the rest remained ignorant of the existence of many other writers, with whose work, in any case, most of us would have been profoundly out of sympathy, because they worshipped at shrines which were not ours: chiefly those of Allen Ginsberg, Charles Olson and William Carlos Williams. No voice reached us from the Pop poets of Liverpool or the Black Mountaineers of Birmingham.

Basil Bunting, buried in a newspaper office in Newcastle, was as completely unknown to us as he was to the more established part of the London literary scene.

When it came to the other arts, the members of the Group had a certain sympathy for music—chiefly through the advocacy of Martin Bell and Peter Porter—but little for the modern visual arts. Mozart, Mahler and Donizetti had their places in our collective pantheon, but the same could not be said for Matisse, Ernst or Picasso. The exploration of modern painting was something that I undertook alone.

I have often wondered just how it is that the visual arts came to play so great a rôle in my life. I had little contact with good painting or sculpture as a child, and I have never wanted to be a painter. In Jamaica, my mother sent me to take a series of lessons with a refugee artist—one of a scattering of 'artistic' Central Europeans who somehow found their way to the West Indies at the height of the war. I remember little about him—a saturnine face, perhaps, and a rakish little beard. I do recall looking at his sculptures, compact figures of deer and other animals carved in coloured marble which I now realize must have been influenced by Gaudier-Brzeska. And I have a memory of myself sitting in his leafy garden and trying to make a watercolour of a single gladiolus stem, with flesh-pink flowers, placed on a rickety three-legged table in an old accumulator-jar. More recently, the memory was confirmed when I found this very drawing while going through an old trunk. The straggly green leaves of the plant were clearly the work of a child, and a bored child at that. the sticky blooms were crisply drawn, and must have been the work of my instructor, anxious to earn his fee by giving me something to take home to my mother. I believe the lessons did not last long, as I was too intractable.

I think it was probably Madame Bonnemaison who first succeeded in making me look at modern paintings seriously. As she herded her charges through the galleries of the Musée de l'Art Moderne, it was always I who exasperated the others by lingering behind for a further look. But the seeds which were then quickening had been planted a long time before—by my childhood in Jamaica, by the tranquil beauty of Canterbury where

I had been at school. I now realize that Jamaica gave me one valuable gift in particular. Because I left it when I did, and felt such a powerful nostalgia for it, I went on trying to remember what everything had looked like; and gradually I built my childhood again in my mind, detail by detail. Insensibly, I thus acquired the techniques of organizing, not thought (such skill as I possess in that I owe to my formal education) but visual sensations. These techniques were to stand me in good stead when I started to write about art.

My early ventures into art criticism happened at Oxford, when I wrote a few reviews for *Isis*. The first was of an exhibition of Bernard Leach's pottery, held at the Beaux-Arts Gallery in 1951. As well as looking at the show, I interviewed Leach himself—the perfect subject, with his idealism and generosity, for the nervous beginner I then was. The reason, of course, why I had been given the job was that at Oxford, too, not many of my contemporaries were interested in art. I knew few, for example, who paid regular visits to the Ashmolean; and in those days, before the advent of the Oxford Gallery and the Museum of Modern Art, undergraduates had little opportunity to see contemporary work. Even the tiny Bear Lane Gallery had not yet come into being.

Settled at last in London, I became an art critic by gradual, almost accidental stages. Every Saturday I used to go to the Portobello Road, where the antique market, though extensive enough, had not as yet grown to the size it is today. And on most of these Saturdays I would lunch at a little café run by three genteel old ladies, who served good home-made bread and home-made soup. The latter was especially welcome on bitter winter days. It did not take me long to make the acquaintance of a small group of other antique-hunters, who were even more assiduous than myself. One of these was an elegant young Swede (though long domiciled in England) of about my own age. We soon became friends, and saw a lot of one another.

One day, I ran into Sven, not in the Portobello, but somewhere in St James's. He seized my arm with the words: 'Just the person I wanted to see! You used to review exhibitions at Oxford, didn't you?' It turned out that he wanted me to take over the reviews he was doing for a paper called *Art News and Review*. The pay in those days was £1 an article, and no expenses. For this, I used to slip out of the office in the afternoons and dash all over London, visiting galleries in the strangest nooks and corners. Many shut their doors after a few months, never to be heard of again. Soon I was writing ten or fifteen reviews an issue, and soon other offers began to come in: to act as alternate on the *New Statesman*, to review for *The Listener*, to appear on the BBC 'Critics'.

The London art world which I entered in this extremely provisional, not to say casual, way, was on the verge of a great transformation. The early fifties had witnessed an extraordinary, and even in its way heroic, attempt to stem the rising tide of abstraction. Abstract art, already triumphant elsewhere, was confronted by a native school of figurative painting, that of the so-called 'kitchen sink' realists. Their principal support among the critics was the Marxist John Berger, who was influential less because of his passionate convictions and his commitment to the cause he had taken up, than because he was by far the most readable and entertaining art reviewer of his time. It was his reviews, as much as the new poems and the articles about new poetry, that I looked for when I read the *New Statesman* in my Oxford Junior Common Room.

In conducting his campaign, Berger could rely on a long-standing national prejudice in favour of figurative art, almost the equivalent of the anti-modernism which possessed so many critics of literature. When, in 1951, he reviewed the *British Abstract Art* exhibition at the Gimpel Fils gallery, he asserted that the movement towards abstraction 'had become a heresy—which is to say an interesting half-truth which threatens the stable but constantly developing main tradition'.

But Berger's assertions would have had little effect unless he had been able to find some countervailing force—artists who based themselves on different principles. Visiting the *Young Contemporaries* show of 1952, he discovered what he was looking for. He said of the young artists whose work he found there that 'taken as a whole, these pictures prove that the majority of the young have a common attitude. This attitude is based upon the everyday and the ordinary.' And he added, 'Their way of look-

ing . . . implies a fresh intention: an intention to discover and
express the reality, the sharper meaning, given to such apparently
unremarkable subjects by the lives and habits of the people they
concern.' These words outline the principles upon which the
counter-attack was to be based. They also prefigure in a remark-
able way the things which Robert Conquest was to say three
years later about the poets he included in *New Lines*.

Though a 'little Englander' by temperament, just as he was a
Marxist by conviction, Berger did not rely entirely upon the work
of a handful of younger British artists (they included Jack Smith,
John Bratby, Derrick Greaves and Edward Middleditch) to prove
his case for him. Unlike the literary critics, he looked abroad,
but in a blinkered way. He found support for his thesis in the
later work of the Franco-Russian painter Nicolas de Staël, at the
period when de Staël turned from abstraction to simplified
figuration; and, predictably, he also found it in the work being
done by Italian Social Realists, notably Renato Guttuso. His dis-
likes, however, were more sweeping, and they were shared by
other influential critics of the time.

Since the great upsurge of the visual arts during the sixties, the
ferocity and tenacity of the British resistance to manifestations
now regarded as 'classic' or nearly so has tended to be forgotten.
I think it is worth quoting one or two judgements upon important artists to show just how stubborn it was. Berger himself made
a violent attack on the Dubuffet show which the Institute of
Contemporary Arts put on in 1955:

> If all the other shows they put on for the rest of the year prove
> to be entirely commendable, the waste of gallery space and
> the abuse of prestige, which lie behind this exhibition, will
> remain unforgivable.

Patrick Heron, by no means such a foe as Berger was to abstract
art in general, made the following comment on a painting by
Jackson Pollock which appeared in another ICA exhibition during
the early fifties:

> Pollock is the inventor of a method now famous: the picture

is made by pouring quick-drying paint on to a horizontal canvas from tins. The result is as mechanical as the method.

But there was something paradoxical about the art world with which I was about to involve myself. The exhibition record of the early fifties tells a different story from the one told by the reviewers. Exhibition organizers offered steady support to many of the things which critics were readiest to abuse, and the shows they put on gradually educated the public. For example, Moore had his first retrospective at the Tate in 1951; Hepworth her first at the Whitechapel Art Gallery in 1954; and there was a Sutherland retrospective at the ICA in 1953. Alan Davie was given his first London showing at Gimpel Fils in 1950; Terry Frost had his at the Leicester Galleries in 1952. British sculptors of a generation younger than that of Moore and Hepworth were active. This was the period when artists such as Lynn Chadwick, Kenneth Armitage, Reg Butler and Bernard Meadows made their reputations. True, the romantic, semi-surrealist style favoured by these artists has now gone out of favour almost as drastically as 'kitchen sink' realism. Yet, unlike the latter, it did represent a real effort to link natively English sentiment and expression to what was going on in Europe.

As the fifties waned it was increasingly clear that big changes were in the making. In 1955, Mark Tobey was given a show at the ICA; and in 1956—the year in which Smith, Middleditch, Bratby and Greaves were chosen to be the British representatives at the Venice Biennale—an exhibition entitled *Modern Art in the United States*, which had been organized by the Museum of Modern Art, New York, arrived at the Tate Gallery. It contained work by most of the leading Abstract Expressionists, including Kline, Rothko and Pollock, and it gave a very considerable jolt to the London art community. I can still remember how raw and shocking the Abstract Expressionist works seemed, and how impossible it was to think of them as paintings in any sense I had hitherto recognized. But at the same time there was a realization (some people found it humiliating) that British art had been living in a kind of fool's paradise, supporting itself with assumptions which were no longer tenable.

More insidious, but almost equally important, was the effect of a show which was put on at the Whitechapel Art Gallery in the same year. Called *This is Tomorrow*, it was the work of a circle of painters, sculptors, architects and critics who dubbed themselves the Independent Group. Among them were Eduardo Paolozzi, Raynor Banham, Alison and Peter Smithson, and Richard Hamilton. The exhibition was planned as an investigation of the possibilities of integrating different arts, but its chief claim to fame seems, in retrospect, to be the fact that it foreshadowed the birth of Pop Art. Hamilton created a collage for it, 'Just what is it that makes today's homes so different, so appealing?' This has been recognized by subsequent chroniclers as the first specimen of Pop, in the sense in which art-critics were later to employ the term.

It is not, I think, putting it too strongly to say that, at the very moment when I arrived on the scene, the critic's function, as well as the art he was called upon to deal with, started to change in a radical way. What now seems quaint about Berger's reviews when I re-read them is not so much their provincialism as the cocky assertiveness of their judgements. The critic still believes that he stands on firm ground. I don't think I've ever had that feeling, in nearly two decades of trying to write about contemporary art. Throughout that period, the critic, so-called, has been no more than the 'village explainer' of Gertrude Stein's phrase—she used it to describe Ezra Pound, adding, 'All right if you are a village; if not, not.'

This is not the place for a capsule history of the art of the late fifties, sixties and seventies, as we have seen it in Britain. What I should like to try to define here is the effect of living, intellectually, in such an entirely provincial situation. In fact, this chapter may be thought of as a kind of letter of explanation, written to my literary friends (who, I suspect, on the whole disapprove of my involvement with contemporary art) on behalf of those artists whose work has fascinated and fed me for more than a decade—I use the verb 'to feed', of course, in its earthiest as well as its most rarefied sense. By some quirk of demand, it is probably easier for a free-lance writer to make a living by writing about art, than by writing about any other form of cultural activity.

But first, a reminder that this has been a period when styles of art have succeeded one another with astonishing rapidity: Abstract Expressionism, Pop Art, Op Art, Kinetic Art, the Art of Assemblage, Post-Painterly Abstraction, Minimalism, Conceptualism, Super Realism. No doubt the litany could be lengthened with one or two other terms of the same type. The resistance put up by Berger and his like also meant that, here in England, the developments I have listed were compressed into an even briefer span of time than they occupied elsewhere.

I have often had it pointed out to me, by friends not committed to the world of modern art, that the fact that something has happened, or been created, is not in itself a guarantee of its artistic quality or enduring interest. This is true. Artists are inclined to try to convince one that the mere existence of an object, or even of an idea or a tendency, is in itself sufficient justification. In the art world, one is told, whatever happens has to be attended to—a democracy of attention is what is required. One has to recognize this for what it is: a defence mechanism in the face of the psychological threat posed by the sheer openness of the art situation.

Yet there is a difference of mental attitude, and I think this can be defined, not in a phrase but in a name: Marcel Duchamp. Duchamp's doctrine of the 'found object'; his conviction that choosing, in certain circumstances, was as good as making, so that a rack for drying bottles could become a piece of sculpture, without physical alteration of any kind, simply because he, Duchamp, said that it was. There is no doubt, first, that Duchamp began by offering the notion ironically; and second, that it is full of pitfalls. For example, it raises the whole question of how we define the artist.

In another sense, however, Duchamp opens a door to the phenomenal world—one returns through him to that purity of attention which the mystics have always set such store by. A shift of light, the fall of a leaf—it seems curious to have travelled by such a winding and difficult road to find that it has conducted one back to some of the perceptions of early childhood.

But I am running too far forward in my account. When I first started to write art criticism I was very naïve. It took me a long time to get my bearings, and I blush to think of how much of my education I conducted in public. My whole career had been designed to unfit me, rather than to fit me, for an understanding of what modern artists were doing. But I was naïve in a cruder sense as well.

For example, I was frightened of Bohemia. I came into collision with this fact in the advertising agency I worked for. One of our senior copywriters had constituted herself the protectress of the two Scottish painters, Robert Colquhoun and Robert MacBryde, who had enjoyed considerable success in the forties, but who were now far gone in idleness and alcoholism. Mostly she met them in the French Pub in Dean Street, then still the headquarters of the old Bohemian world, which had moved a fraction southwards from its original haunts in Fitzrovia. But she also, whenever she could, smuggled them back into the agency after working hours. She was determined that the rest of us should love and respect them as much as she did herself.

I suspect that 'the two Roberts', as they were called, found these confrontations as uncomfortable as we did. Miss Richards would be rushing around, talking incessantly, searching for a hidden bottle of claret, a corkscrew, and some moderately clean glasses. Meanwhile, her two protégés, stranded in the bright fluorescent glare of our top-floor studios, like a pair of fish on a fishmonger's slab, would slowly lose whatever animation they had possessed when they arrived. Colquhoun's gaunt, putty-coloured face, with its stubble of whisker, gradually slackened, so that his mouth gaped, showing a row of ruined yellow teeth behind the lower lip. He seemed, even if one had wanted to approach him, utterly unreachable.

Colquhoun and MacBryde are now both dead, but I think that if I met them now I should feel compassion as well as fear. If they threw away the talents they possessed, they were encouraged to do so by the expectations about the artist, and the behaviour of artists, with which they grew up. A formula was imposed upon them, and they accepted it.

Of course, the Bohemian formula was to be replaced by others, and that was part of the change that the sixties brought with it. For a moment, it seemed that the Bohemia which artists such as these represented was precisely the thing which the new vigorous British art world was determined to blot out of its collective consciousness. The tone was set by the rise of Pop Art, and by the link which was rapidly forged between the art mafia and other representatives of the 'swinging London' of the early sixties. Now that swinging London has vanished, like the mirage it always was, it is easy to condemn it. Soon, no doubt, it will seem, not only as vulgar, but as inherently improbable, as the golden Daimler cars which Sir Bernard and Lady Docker used to commission for themselves a little earlier. And it did seem, at one point, as if, in obliterating the Bohemian myth, it would replace it with one just as damaging to those who believed in it.

This was the myth of the artist as playboy, able to command all the toys and trinkets of a materialistic urban civilization, to manipulate its clichés to his own advantage, and without damage to his gift. There was a good deal of glib talk about the need to accept the essential 'ephemerality' of the art being produced by a new generation of *Wunderkinder*, but my suspicion was that nobody believed it, any more than the Italian Futurists of the years before the First World War believed that they would soon be outdated, while proclaiming the fact in their manifestos. Yet we ought to have been able to foresee that numb weariness which would inevitably be the nemesis of an art which wedded itself so firmly to the notion of success as the only justification and the only good. Whether one foresaw it or not, it has now overtaken the world which Pop Art and its camp-followers created.

Yet how amusing and also how liberating that world seemed at the time! The solemnity of the literary New Left was here answered with impertinence and laughter. Because I still worked in advertising, I was well placed to savour the cogency of the answers which art seemed to be making to the things I found repressive in literature. If painters were justified in making pictures which were about advertisements, girlie-magazines, commercial packaging and characters from popular comic strips, why must we poets bow to critics who seemed to feel that the thing for us to do was to refurbish the eternal verities of the English countryside for our largely urban audiences?

Since the heyday of Pop Art, there have been various other

attempts to define the rôle of the artist. In abstract art, we have
been offered the morality of process, where everything must be
referred to its function within the closed system of the painting
or the piece of sculpture. The rest of the world can go hang: the
artificially created universe, though so little, both in its dimen-
sions and in its ambitions, is held to exclude all consideration of
the natural one.

More recently, conceptual artists, basing themselves on a per-
version of Duchampian doctrine, have asserted their right to
present an 'immaterial' art—that is, an art where the idea is all,
and the physical embodiment almost irrelevant. This shows a
magpie determination to plunder other disciplines. But the artist
as philosopher or the artist as scientist is seldom equipped for the
tasks he so lightly undertakes. If an exhibition consists of a series
of statements about St Thomas Aquinas, pinned up round the
walls of a gallery, is it too much to ask that they make as much
sense as a collection of statements about the same subject which
one might find in a book? Yet if one poses this question one is
denounced as a spoil-sport. Intellectual lacunae are filled in and
justified by the impalpable presence of the intention to make art.

How can I justify my attachment to a profession whose
foundations I find unstable, and to a world whose experiments I
cannot resist ridiculing? I think I can only do so by returning to
that notion of freedom, of the liberty both to see and to feel,
which is the point at which modern art seems to differ from the
fundamental assumptions of the world in which I grew up. In me,
perhaps a little more than in most people, the processes of experience and emotion are inextricable. To recount the experience
is to re-create the emotion, and that is what I have tried to do in
this book. And it is sights seen as much as actions undertaken
which speak in memory. The burnt child fears the fire, but is still
ravished by the image of it burning.